Exploring Space

Revised Edition

DISCOVERY & EXPLORATION

DISCOVERY & EXPLORATION

Exploring Space
Revised Edition

RODNEY P. CARLISLE

JOHN S. BOWMAN and MAURICE ISSERMAN
General Editors

CHELSEA HOUSE
P U B L I S H E R S
An imprint of Infobase Publishing

Exploring Space, Revised Edition

Copyright ©2010 by Infobase Publishing

Chelsea House
An imprint of Infobase Publishing
132 West 31st Street
New York NY 10001

Library of Congress Cataloging-in-Publication Data
Carlisle, Rodney P.
 Exploring space / Rodney P. Carlisle. -- Rev. ed.
     p. cm. -- (Discovery and exploration)
 Includes bibliographical references and index.
 ISBN 978-1-60413-188-8 (hardcover)
 1. Astronautics--Juvenile literature. 2. Outer space--Exploration--Juvenile literature.
I. Title. II. Series.

 TL793.C363 2010
 629.4--dc22   2009025585

Chelsea House books are available at special discounts when purchased in bulk
quantities for businesses, associations, institutions, or sales promotions. Please call
our Special Sales Department in New York at (212) 967-8800 or (800) 322-8755.

You can find Chelsea House on the World Wide Web at
http://www.chelseahouse.com

Text design by Erika K. Arroyo
Cover design by Keith Trego
Composition by EJB Publishing Services
Cover printed by Bang Printing, Brainerd, MN
Book printed and bound by Bang Printing, Brainerd, MN
Date printed: December 2009
Printed in the United States of America

10 9 8 7 6 5 4 3 2 1

This book is printed on acid-free paper.

All links and Web addresses were checked and verified to be correct at the time of
publication. Because of the dynamic nature of the Web, some addresses and links may
have changed since publication and may no longer be valid.

Contents

1

"Houston, We've Had a Problem"

The day was April 13, 1970. Astronauts James (Jim) Lovell Jr., Fred Haise, and John (Jack) Swigert had finished their first television broadcast from space while moving at more than 2,000 miles (3,218 kilometers) per hour in *Apollo 13*, the United States' fifth mission to the Moon.

On instructions from ground control in Houston, Swigert threw a switch to stir one of the oxygen tanks. A mysterious explosion rocked the spacecraft. Some of the walls buckled with a shudder and a whump. The lights in the craft flickered and went dim. Some instruments went out. The spaceship's fuel immediately sank to dangerous levels, and the ship spun in a tumbling roll. Glancing out the window, the astronauts saw a cloud of gas and debris surrounding the ship. Lovell, his voice disarmingly calm, radioed command center: "Houston, we've had a problem."

Within minutes, both the team on the ground and the astronauts aboard the craft decided that the only way to keep the three alive was to abandon the main ship. The astronauts would move into the tiny lunar module (LM; also called lunar excursion module, or LEM). It was named *Aquarius*, after the mythological water carrier.

Besides the astronauts, there were three shifts of controllers in Houston, as well as the dozens of other engineers and technicians who provided support to the space program in manufacturing companies and for the National Aeronautics and Space Administration (NASA). Immediately, everyone understood that the mission to the Moon had to be cancelled. The astronauts, however, had flown only a small fraction of the 238,000 miles (383,023 km) to the Moon. They would have to loop around the Moon and use its gravity to slingshot them back to Earth. The trip would take four days. Whether they would survive depended on how well they and Houston reacted.

LIFE OR DEATH

The LM was designed to house two men for two days on the Moon. There was enough food aboard the command module *Odyssey* that could be moved down the tunnel to *Aquarius.* More essential requirements were in short supply: water, breathable air, and the crucial supply of electric power to operate the craft. Electricity from batteries controlled the steering and thruster nozzles and kept communications with those on Earth open.

Left to right: Commander Jim Lovell, copilot Thomas K. Mattingly, and lunar module pilot Fred W. Haise pose for a publicity shot before the *Apollo 13* mission. Mattingly was scrubbed from the flight because he had been exposed to measles. He was replaced by Jack Swigert.

The next four days were a round-the-clock struggle. The astronauts and the flight control team in Houston faced dozens of crises. The breathable air aboard the spacecraft became overloaded with exhaled carbon dioxide (CO_2). As the level of concentration of carbon dioxide rose, it could impair judgment and create dizziness. It could even lead to suffocation. To conserve power, electrical systems were shut down. This caused the temperature inside the craft to drop to near-freezing levels. It was nearly impossible to sleep. There also were dangerous amounts of moisture on electrical instrument panels and wiring. Ejection of human waste was cancelled, with the urine stored in plastic sacks.

To conserve water, rations were cut back. If water intake went below six ounces a day, however, it could lead to buildup of toxins in the body. (The normal adult consumption is about 36 ounces a day.) Haise began to suffer symptoms of such poisoning long before the ship approached Earth's atmosphere.

Another concern was the angle of reentry, which had to be carefully adjusted. Too shallow an angle would cause the spacecraft to bounce off the atmosphere like a stone skipped atop a pond of water. Too steep an angle would burn the ship and its contents to a cinder from the friction of the air. The weight of the reentry capsule was another problem. The LM was designed to carry moon rocks on its return. Without the rocks, it was too light. The men loaded the capsule with cameras and other heavy equipment that normally would have been abandoned in space had the mission been successful. The trajectory toward Earth had to be corrected with tiny thruster bursts from the LM, which was not designed to make mid-course changes for the linked three modules.

Sometimes the solution to one problem led to other problems. If carbon dioxide poisoning or toxic levels from limited drinking water disabled the astronauts, they would be unable to execute necessary maneuvers. If power consumption of the electrical systems drained the supply too fast, the parachutes might not deploy.

The astronauts were in a life or death situation. Like earlier explorers, they needed human ingenuity, inventiveness, and courage. Unlike earlier explorers, however, the story of Lovell, Swigert, and Haise was immediately known throughout the world. Television and radio carried the news to millions of viewers and listeners. Everywhere, witnesses

DISTANCE AND TIME

Apollo 13's planned loop around the Moon and back to Earth would be a long and risky trip in the history of exploration. The distance from Earth to the Moon is about 240,000 miles (386,242 km). The exact distance varies because the path of the Moon around Earth is an ellipse, not a circle. At its closest approach to Earth, the Moon is about 216,420 miles (348,294 km) away. The *Apollo* spacecraft, however, made orbits around the Moon, rather than direct surface-to-surface flights. When Christopher Columbus sailed to the Bahamas, Cuba, and Hispaniola and back to Spain in 1492, the distance traveled was less than 10,000 miles (16,093 km). When Sebastian del Cano (who took over the *Victoria* after the death of Ferdinand Magellan) completed the circumnavigation of Earth in 1522, he had traveled 42,000 miles (67,592 km), counting their long routes around South America and Africa. His trip took nearly three years. In 1970, for the *Apollo 13* crew, if all went well after the accident, the nearly half-million-mile (804,672-km) round trip would take four days.

hung on every word of the astronauts' fight for life. In Times Square, New York City, the news ticker kept crowds informed of the astronauts' plight. In St. Peters' Square in Rome, hundreds of thousands offered prayers for their safe return. In Florida, the families of the astronauts gathered, comforting one another. Many feared that Lovell, Swigert, and Haise might not return home alive. The world wondered whether their craft would become a forever-orbiting coffin.

FROM MEDIA BLACKOUT TO MEDIA BLITZ

When the flight had first started, the news media had almost ignored it. No major news channel or network had carried the television broadcast from space. Lovell's wife, Marilyn, and their children had gone to NASA's offices at Cape Canaveral, Florida, to view it because it was not aired on local television. *Aquarius* was the fifth mission to the Moon. The American public had become so used to the concept of space travel, it had become almost routine. However, with the explosion aboard *Apollo 13*, public interest and media attention exploded as well.

For NASA, public attention was important. Founded by an act of Congress on October 1, 1958, NASA represented an effort to put together in a single civilian agency, programs in aeronautics and in space research. As the agency took on responsibility for manned space travel and as rocket launchings drew close television coverage, NASA needed to maintain a good public image. And, as a government agency, it depended on support from lawmakers in Washington and the U.S. voting public. So, the lack of attention from the media at the beginning of the flight was a huge disappointment, not only to the families of the astronauts but also to NASA administrators. Too much attention on the troubles of *Apollo 13* could be disastrous, however. If the three astronauts died on the mission, the tragedy could create a political and funding crisis. It might mean the end of NASA itself.

HOUSTON AT WORK

The flight control team in Houston was headed by Eugene (Gene) F. Kranz. He signed on and off the radio as "Flight," for "flight director." Kranz worked in a control room with banks of computer screens. At each screen, specialists monitored different aspects of the mission. Each specialist had a cryptic name: GUIDO, or guidance officer; INCO, or instrumentation and communications officer; FIDO, or flight dynamics officer; RETRO, or retrofire officer; EECOM, or electrical and environmental command officer; and TELMU, or telemetry, electrical and extravehicular activity mobility unit officer. Other specialists monitored the astronauts' health. Some diagnosed mechanical problems. Some calculated resources consumed. Some worked on the spacecraft trajectory.

Kranz was supported by the prior flight director, Christopher Kraft. He also received advice from other astronauts serving as capsule communicators (CapComs), such as Donald (Deke) Slayton. At one point, Lovell, aboard the spacecraft, grew impatient for the guidance commands for reentry. Kraft had Slayton speak directly with Lovell. Slayton reassured him that they were working on the guidance commands. When Slayton or another astronaut CapCom spoke directly to Lovell, it helped relieve tension.

Beginning with the spacecraft's countdown on the launch tower until the time it lands back on Earth, the Mission Control Center is in charge of overseeing mission operations. At the Houston Command Center, the staff was able to view broadcasts from space as *Apollo 13* reported in. Last used in 1992, the Houston Command Center is now listed in the National Register of Historic Places.

Another ground-based astronaut was Thomas K. (Ken) Mattingly. Mattingly had originally been scheduled to fly aboard *Apollo 13*, but had been bumped at the last minute because he had been exposed to measles by another astronaut. Doctors discovered that he was not immune to the disease and feared he would become ill during the mission. Over Lovell's objections, Mattingly was replaced by Swigert.

Disgruntled, Mattingly had to sit out the flight. However, when the crisis developed aboard *Apollo 13*, Mattingly was recalled to work in the flight simulator. There he tested different ways to shut down pieces of equipment and helped develop the procedures for reentry. Having the originally scheduled *Apollo 13* LM pilot on the ground was a lucky break after all. Mattingly had hundreds of hours of experience in the simulator and a close knowledge of the craft's capabilities. The fact that Lovell knew and trusted Mattingly, that Mattingly was a close member of the team, and that he understood the LM so thoroughly meant that his calculations of reentry procedures were accepted as right on the mark.

Perhaps the most striking case of adaptation under pressure was the ground crew's solution to the problem of carbon dioxide poisoning. Both the LM *Aquarius* and the command module *Odyssey* had CO_2 scrubbers. These had canisters filled with lithium hydroxide that would filter the CO_2 out of the air. Monitors used a mercury readout to determine the level of CO_2. The correct reading should be two or three millimeters of mercury. When the level reached seven millimeters, the astronauts were to change the canisters on their scrubbers. If the level rose above 15, the astronauts would die of carbon dioxide poisoning.

The small scrubber in the LM could not remove all the gas from the air, however. The larger canister from the command module scrubber could do the job, but it had to be connected to the air system in the LM. Designers had made the two scrubbers completely differently, with the command module scrubber canister in a large square box. The LM scrubber canister was made for a smaller, round fitting.

A ground team headed by Robert (Ed) Smylie worked on a solution. Using the same equipment found on the spacecraft—including cooling tubing from underwear worn under the space suits while walking on the Moon, and a flexible cover taken off a loose-leaf binder flight plan— Smylie's designers put together an invention that adapted the command module scrubber filter to the smaller LM connections.

On the LM, Lovell and Swigert tried to nap. The readings on the CO_2 monitor climbed to 13. This was dangerously close to the poisoning mark. Lovell and Swigert joined Haise in gathering the materials needed to make Smylie's contraption: scissors, duct tape, flight-book covers, command module canisters, and tubing. The team aboard *Aquarius* followed Smylie's step-by-step instructions, carefully piecing together the parts.

The astronauts turned on the scrubber. After a few anxious moments, the odd little duct-taped gadget began to work. The mercury level on the CO_2 monitor fell to 12, then down to 10 and below.

After the lunar module's safe landing just a few hundred yards away from U.S. Navy ships, the *Apollo 13* crew were onboard the *Iwo Jima* within 45 minutes. Here, they step down from the rescue helicopter aboard the *Iwo Jima*.

SPLASHDOWN

One by one, the technical problems were solved on the ground and in space by the astronauts. Haise was now suffering from a fever, and all three astronauts were exhausted from interrupted sleep and freezing temperatures. The men transferred back into the command module, *Odyssey*, to use it as a descent capsule. Separating the modules, the three said good-bye to the LM that had been their home for more than three days. Then, they separated the command module from the damaged service module. The service module is where the original explosion had occurred. The crew watched as it slowly turned away into space. Only then could they see its blown-out side. It became clear that an oxygen tank had blown up, probably caused by a bad electrical connection in the machine in the tank that was to stir the oxygen. The astronauts hurriedly snapped a few photographs of the damaged service module before returning to their stations for reentry.

Slanting into the atmosphere at some 25,000 miles (40,233 km) per hour, the heat shield on the base of the *Odyssey* module heated up to 5,000° Fahrenheit (2,760° Celsius) or more. It broke the air into a radiation shower of ions (charged subatomic particles) as it streaked toward its splashdown site in the Pacific Ocean. Below on Earth, listeners waited through a minute of radio silence, as communications were broken by the heat shield's ion burst. If the shield broke, the ship would disintegrate, and the astronauts would burn to death.

Nervously, CapCom Joseph (Joe) Kerwin radioed: "*Odyssey*, Houston standing by, over." The seconds ticked by with no response. The message repeated: "*Odyssey*, Houston standing by, over." No response.

Then the static level changed, and Swigert's voice came on. He responded, "OK, Joe." The assembled team broke into applause. Around the world, the words were relayed. Millions of people listening to the radio and watching the television heaved a sigh of relief. Minutes later, the spacecraft's first small parachutes opened. The small parachutes were designed to pull out larger ones that, in turn, pulled out the three main parachutes. These main parachutes floated the capsule at a gentle 20 miles (32 km) per hour down to the ocean, a few hundred yards away from waiting U.S. Navy ships.

A helicopter lifted the astronauts from the sea. They were safe. Space travel had shown that exploration continued to require brave individuals. Explorers of space would risk their lives, just as explorers on land and sea had done before them.

2

Exploring the Universe
From Ptolemy to
Newton and Beyond

LONG BEFORE THE FIRST ROCKETS LIFTED PEOPLE INTO SPACE, humans explored the universe without leaving Earth. In the centuries before electric light, the starry skies were a spectacular display of light. The stars fascinated wise men, priests, and ordinary people. For observers in the Northern Hemisphere, the stars seemed to rotate slowly in the heavens around an imaginary point that was due north.

EXPLORING THE NIGHT SKY
BEFORE TELESCOPES

People had many questions about the way the night sky looked. What were the stars? How far away were they? Why did some steady spots of light appear to wander from night to night? Did the constellations, or patterns, of the stars have any special meaning? Babylonian observers called the string of constellations the Zodiac. They named the twelve constellations, in groups of three, depending on the season. The dots of light in each constellation, when connected with imaginary lines, made up the outlines of mythical beings. They ranged from Aries (the Ram) and Taurus (the Bull) to Aquarius (the Waterbearer), and Pisces (the Fishes).

The ancient Babylonians next invented the magical concept of astrology. Astrologers predicted the influence of the stars on a person's life. Today, astrology lives on; however, modern science rejects its logic. But on a clear night, modern sky watchers can still see the same constellations identified thousands of years ago.

The ancient astrologers collected details about the stars. They named the constellations and many of the brightest stars. They also tracked the paths of the planets that they could see: Mercury, Venus, Mars, Jupiter, and Saturn. The exploration of the universe had begun. Still, its meaning and the way it worked remained full of mystery.

Some early space explorers sought rational, rather than mystical, answers to their questions. They used the tools of logic, mathematics, and physics. One theory was developed by a Greek astronomer living in Egypt. Claudius Ptolemy (A.D. 100–170) took into account the motions of the planets and the stars. He reasoned that something in the sky had to be holding up the stars. He proposed invisible spheres, one nested inside the other, carried the stars and planets. The spheres rotated about Earth, he explained. The planets, the Sun, and the Moon were each on a different sphere, spinning around Earth. Earth, Ptolemy believed, was at the center of the universe, standing still.

Ptolemy's theory made sense: It certainly appeared that Earth stood still. It also appeared as if the Sun, the Moon, and the stars moved across the sky. The invisible spheres holding up the stars also seemed to be sensible. What else kept them from falling out of the sky? Ptolemy's theory was convincing because it was based on evidence, including his own observations. Many people accepted Ptolemy's explanation for more than 1,500 years, adding minor changes to his ideas to explain new details and contradictions.

FIRST EXPLORATION WITH THE TELESCOPE

Sometime between A.D. 1280 and 1286, an inventor made the first eyeglasses. The inventor probably worked in or near Venice, Italy. Within 20 years, people across Europe were wearing glasses to improve their eyesight. About 300 years later, an eyeglass lens maker, Hans Lippershey of Holland, made a discovery. He mounted two lenses in a line. This let him magnify far away objects. Lippershey made the first telescope in 1608. Word of his idea spread rapidly from country to country.

In Italy, Galileo Galilei (1564–1642), math professor at the University of Padua, heard of the telescope and built one for himself. Galileo was the first to explore the universe with the telescope. He turned it first on the Moon, then he studied the planets. He found a number of new

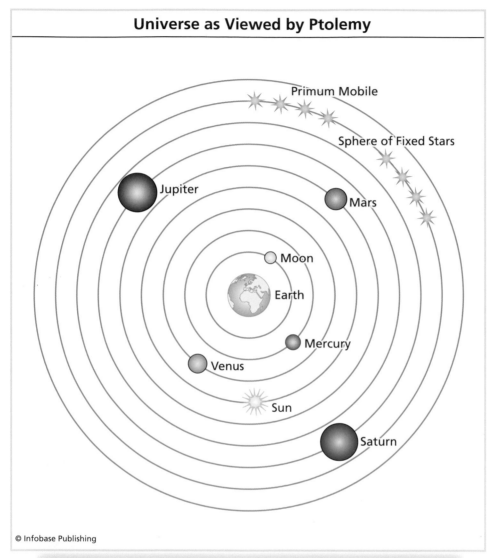

Universe as Viewed by Ptolemy

Primum Mobile

Sphere of Fixed Stars

Jupiter

Mars

Moon

Earth

Mercury

Venus

Sun

Saturn

© Infobase Publishing

Claudius Ptolemy was an astronomer, mathematician, and geographer. Ptolemy reasoned that the stars and the planets stayed in the sky due to a series of crystalline spheres. He believed that the planets as well as the Sun and the Moon passed on different pathways around Earth, which was at the center of the universe.

and exciting facts. Although astronomers had assumed all objects in the heavens to be made of "heavenly," or perfect, material, he found that the Moon was covered with mountains and craters and what appeared to be dark seas. Furthermore, he found that Venus, assumed to be a perfect disk of light, was in fact like the Moon in that it had phases. Jupiter, he discovered, was surrounded by four small moons that rotated around it. The Sun itself had sunspots that moved across the face of the Sun, either from the Sun's own movement or the movement of Earth. Galileo reported his discoveries in a short publication, *Siderius Nuncius* (Starry Messenger), in March 1610.

The discoveries of Galileo came at just the right time. More than 60 years before, in 1543, Nicolaus Copernicus (1473–1543), had suggested that Ptolemy's view of the universe with Earth at the center might be wrong. Copernicus, a Polish churchman and scientist, believed the Sun was at the center of the universe and Earth and the other planets rotated around it. He believed in a heliocentric (Sun-centered) system. Ptolemy's theory supported a geocentric (Earth-centered) system. The two systems were under debate when Galileo published his observations. Some thought the heliocentric idea explained the odd motions of the planets better. Others thought it flew in the face of accepted astronomy and that it even contradicted statements in the Bible.

Several facts made Galileo's study even more controversial. For one thing, the 1543 edition of Copernicus's *De revolutionibus* included a disclaimer suggesting that the heliocentric view was simply an alternative explanation, not an assertion that Copernicus was right or that Ptolemy was wrong. In 1610, however, Galileo was now offering some facts that backed up heliocentrism as not just an alternative but a better explanation. Perhaps the most striking aspect of his discoveries was that Jupiter, like Earth, had its own moons. Furthermore, the mountains on the Moon suggested that heaven and Earth were more similar than anyone had supposed. Much of the exploration and discovery from the telescope seemed to support the new and controversial ideas of Copernicus.

Galileo loved to argue, and he was a master of "disputation." This was a method of teaching that set one view against another. He was good at it and really enjoyed putting down his opponents. As a consequence, he left a trail of hurt feelings. Some people looked for a chance to discredit him. Galileo also ran into problems with the Catholic Church. The Roman Catholic Church had become increasingly concerned about challenges to its established views. Some of those challenges came from the rise of Protestantism, and some came out of the findings and speculations of scientists. Among the well-established premises of the church was that Earth stood still. Many Catholics believed this theory was supported by various phrases in the Bible.

Several of Galileo's enemies reported him to the Catholic Church. He was summoned to Rome to face possible charges of heresy. Heresy, or disagreement with church doctrine, was a crime punishable by death. Galileo pointed out that he had not intended to challenge the church's views. He was told that he should not publish anything that went against established teachings on the subject. He promised to obey.

In 1632, he published a work that explored the controversy. The *Dialogue on Two World Systems* was written in the form of a debate. Widely distributed, the book described each side of the argument. At the end of the book, an "independent" judge decided which theory was correct. The conclusion of the judge was that the traditional view was correct. Galileo thought this meant the book could be viewed as not challenging the church. A couple of church censors even officially stamped it with their seal of approval.

Nevertheless, Galileo was a bit too clever for his own good. Although he had made the book appear to be formally favoring the traditional view, if one read between the lines, one could see that the arguments in favor of the Copernican heliocentric view came across as better than the Catholic Church's preferred Ptolemaic view. It was clear to many readers that Galileo had tried to outwit the church.

Galileo was called to Rome again and tried for heresy. He was convicted and sentenced to house arrest in 1633. For the rest of his life, he was confined to his home. By the standards of the day, he got off lightly. Many others who were convicted of heresy were executed by being burned at the stake. Some were killed by other gruesome methods. In this way, exploration of space by telescope got off to a risky start.

EXPLORING BY TELESCOPE AFTER GALILEO

Over the following centuries, more astronomers began to use telescopes to expand their knowledge of the universe. They made discoveries that were built on the findings of Galileo. Others built improved telescopes that were more compact and had better resolution and focus and higher magnification. Most astronomers had come to accept the view of Copernicus and Galileo that the planets revolved around the

Sun. Fortunately, now these ideas could be explored without threat of torture or execution.

Isaac Newton (1642–1727), an English physicist and mathematician, invented a telescope that had a side aperture and a mirror system. It allowed him to use a shorter length tube for the same degree of magnification as a much longer telescope. Telescopes of that design were later called Newtonian telescopes. Even more important, Newton worked out the basic principles of gravity and the laws of motion. These explained how the planets revolved without falling from the sky and how Earth continued in its orbit around the Sun.

Over the next 250 years, the exploration of the universe by telescope resulted in one discovery after another. Astronomers who built their own telescopes and their own observatories made many of the discoveries. It is a tradition that continues today. Many amateur astronomers practice rooftop and backyard astronomy.

FINDING NEW PLANETS

The spacing of the planets from one another and the Sun puzzled these early explorers of space. A German astronomer, Johann Daniel Titius (1729–1796), in 1766, proposed a formula that showed a mathematical pattern for the distances between the planets and the Sun. A fellow German, Johann Elert Bode (1747–1826), popularized the formula in 1772 and later. The idea came to be known as the Titius-Bode law, or Bode's law. According to the Titius-Bode law, there should have been a planet between Mars and Jupiter and another undiscovered planet orbiting around the Sun at a distance equal to about 19.6 times the distance from the Sun to Earth. Actually, there was no planet between Mars and Jupiter, but there was a group of small objects in orbit there, called asteroids. The discovery of the fairly large asteroid Ceres in 1801 by the Italian astronomer Giuseppe Piazzi (1746–1826) could be taken to fulfill the Titius-Bode law.

Even more exciting was the earlier discovery of the planet Uranus in 1781 by British astronomer William Herschel (1738–1822). Herschel had discovered Uranus through a survey with a large telescope that he had built himself. He spotted an object that clearly was not a star. At first he assumed that he had found a new comet. He later confirmed that it was the seventh planet from the Sun. Uranus was the first planet to be discovered

English scientist Isaac Newton built the first ever reflecting telescope in 1668. His invention had a side aperture and a mirror system that allowed for the same degree of magnification as a much longer telescope. The two types of telescopes used today were developed by Newton (the reflector) and Galileo (the refractor).

by telescope. The other six had all been known since ancient times, found by the first astrologers of Babylon and others who had explored with the naked eye. Once Herschel found Uranus, observers noticed that it is actually bright enough to be identified without a telescope. With the unaided eye, it can be seen as a faint speck, but it was just so obscure and small that no one had noticed its motion against the background of stars before. Herschel planned to name his discovery *Georgium Sidus*, or Georgian star, after King George III of England. Others thought that the planet should be named in the discoverer's honor. German astronomer Johann Elert Bode suggested the name Uranus. Uranus was a mythological figure who was the father of Saturn. The name stuck.

Herschel also discovered the two largest satellites of Uranus—Titania and Oberon—in 1787. In other discoveries, Herschel found two moons of Saturn. He began a method of statistical astronomy, building up star counts for different parts of the night sky. In addition, this telescope-explorer proved that the Sun itself was in motion.

Astronomers studied the orbit of Uranus. They calculated that it was affected by another large, undiscovered planet. These calculations led, in 1846, to the discovery of the planet Neptune by German astronomer Johann G. Galle (1812–1910). The discovery of Neptune through mathematical calculation was one of the great accomplishments of nineteenth-century celestial mechanics. In Berlin, Galle made the first actual sighting of the planet, using his telescope as well as the calculations.

As telescopes grew larger and more expensive, new ones were built by institutions and universities. Soon, the distinction between professional astronomers and amateurs grew. Still, both groups continued to explore and make discoveries. One who crossed the line between amateur and professional was Percival Lowell (1855–1916). Lowell, an American, spent some of his personal fortune to build an observatory in Flagstaff, Arizona, in 1894. Lowell studied the surface of Mars and observed areas thought to be canals. He came up with a whole theory of a system of irrigation canals. He thought these canals carried water from the polar regions to cities in the desert. Alfred Wallace (1823–1913), a respected British engineer and naturalist, challenged Lowell's view. Wallace showed that the temperatures on Mars were well below the freezing point of water. The atmosphere was too thin for Earth-like life. Later spacecraft exploration proved Wallace right and Lowell wrong.

One of the greatest advances in the frontier of space came from a professional American astronomer, Edwin Powell Hubble (1889–1953). Hubble discovered that beyond Earth's galaxy (the Milky Way) were thousands of other galaxies. Each galaxy was made up of many stars. Hubble introduced in 1925 a classification of the galaxies as different

LIFE ON OTHER PLANETS

Nicolaus Copernicus proposed and Galileo Galilei confirmed that other planets were not simply light sources. They were made of rock and solid like Earth. Scientists speculated almost immediately that there might be life on the other planets. In 1593, an Italian, Giordano Bruno (1548–1600), suggested there might be hundreds of other planets with life like Earth. He was tried for heresy and burned at the stake in 1600. But times changed. In 1877, Giovanni Schiaparelli (1835–1910), an Italian astronomer, drew a picture of the surface of Mars. He identified dark streaks on the surface as *canali,* the Italian word for "grooves." Word of his findings spread and created excitement. In English, the word *canali* can be translated as "canals." Of course, on Earth a canal is a human-made feature, not a natural crack or riverbed. For most of the next century, the idea of canals on Mars inspired hundreds of science fiction stories. American astronomer Percival Lowell strongly believed that Mars was inhabited. Many others were eager to believe that intelligent beings lived on this nearby planet.

Other astronomers had trouble spotting the canals that Schiaparelli had seen. Most professional astronomers concluded by the 1930s that the lines seen by Schiaparelli were optical effects, not true markings on the surface. All agreed, however, that Mars had some interesting features that could support life. They found white ice caps at the northern and southern poles that grew and receded with the seasons. Someday, science fiction fans believed, humans would meet the Martians.

types: spirals, barred spirals, lenticular, irregular, and ellipticals. Hubble also calculated that the universe was expanding.

By the time Hubble published his theories, Russian, German, and American engineers began the first experiments with rockets that would have the potential to visit outer space. The next stage of space exploration was about to begin.

3

First Steps to Space
Germans, Soviets, and Americans

ALTHOUGH SOLID-FUELED ROCKETS HAVE EXISTED AS WEAPONS since their invention in China in the twelfth century A.D., the use of rockets for the exploration of space was a twentieth-century invention. In the mid-1920s, the idea of using rockets for spaceships was subject matter for science fiction books. By the 1950s, these ideas had become reality. They moved to engineers' drawing boards and full-scale production.

Both amateurs and professionals played key roles in these developments. A series of inventions resulted in successful rockets. They launched payloads into orbit around Earth, and then the rockets were on their way to the Moon. The first rocket designers were an interesting bunch. They included mathematics teachers, filmmakers and writers, mechanics, engineers, and army artillery officers. At first, there were only a few scientists with graduate degrees in physics and other fields involved in rocketry.

These groups of rocket enthusiasts moved from forming clubs and societies to working with government assistance. Soon, rocket science was a recognized profession. All of this happened in one short generation. Out of these developments grew several corporations in the United States (and later in other countries) that made rockets for space exploration. In the Soviet Union, state agencies formed out of the same kind of backgrounds, pioneering the way to space by the 1950s.

EARLY SOVIET AND GERMAN ROCKET RESEARCH

Konstantin Tsiolkovsky (1857–1935) was one of the first believers in space travel by rocket. He worked as a high school math teacher in the Russian town of Kaluga, about 100 miles (160.9 km) from Moscow. He planned rockets as early as 1895. In 1898, he published the first of three articles suggesting how to build such rockets. One of his works, "Exploration of Cosmic Space by Reactive Devices," was published in 1903. This article foresaw the future of rocket space exploration.

Another math teacher who became interested in space travel was Hermann Oberth (1894–1989). Oberth, who lived in Romania, began studying rockets after World War I. He suggested mixing gasoline or kerosene with liquid oxygen. This, he believed, would give far more lift than a rocket fueled by gunpowder or smokeless powder. He thought that this fuel could put a space station in orbit. He visualized orbiting platforms with huge mirrors that could focus the Sun's rays to melt ice in northern ports on Earth. Oberth wrote and published, in 1923, a small pamphlet that summarized his concepts. His little pamphlet received a lot of attention.

Others in the Soviet Union had similar ideas. Fridrikh Tsander (1887–1933) was an engineer from Latvia. He began giving lectures on space flight. Tsander formed an amateur club, the Society for the Study of Interplanetary Communication, in 1924. Tsander's group put on a public exhibition in Moscow in 1927. It attracted the attention of Sergei Korolev (1906–1966). Korolev had attended technical school in Kiev and Moscow in the Soviet Union. He met Tsiolkovsky in 1927 and Tsander in 1930. Tsander and Korolev helped found the Moscow Group for the Study of Reaction Motion (MosGIRD). Members joked that the Russian initials of the group also stood for Moscow Group of Engineers Working for Nothing.

Meanwhile, the Soviet army had become interested in rockets. Rocket scientist Valentin Glushko (1908–1989) set up an army research group in Leningrad (now St. Petersburg). In 1932, Glushko built the first liquid rocket engine to fire successfully. It burned gasoline and liquid oxygen and produced 44 pounds of thrust. Soon the army supported the work of the GIRD group in Moscow. In 1933, a

GIRD rocket climbed to 1,300 feet (396 meters) before crashing. Later that year, the GIRD group moved out of their borrowed basement into a true test facility in a former diesel engine factory outside Moscow. Korolev joined the army and was made an officer.

In Germany, as in the Soviet Union, amateurs started rocket research. Austrian movie producer Fritz Lang worked on a science fiction movie, *Girl in the Moon*. He hired Oberth as a consultant. Oberth convinced Lang that he should build a real rocket. An engineer, Rudolf Nebel (1894–1978), joined the team. Oberth worked with a club, the Verein fur Raumshiffahrt (VfR, or Society for Space Travel), that raised funds. Eventually the German army noticed the efforts run by Oberth and Nebel and provided some small grants.

The VfR recruited people with all sorts of backgrounds, including Wernher von Braun (1912–1977), a young aristocrat. Von Braun joined Nebel's group and began studies toward a doctorate with army support. By 1934, with army funding, von Braun and colleagues from the VfR built the A-1 rocket. According to von Braun, it took a half year to build and a half second to blow up. However, the team kept at it. They launched an A-2 that flew in December 1934 up to one mile (1.6 km) in altitude. In 1936, von Braun convinced the army to pay for an elaborate test facility on the Baltic Sea.

Each von Braun design was an improvement over the other, concluding in the A-4. The A-4 rocket had a system of changing the direction of thrust of the motors. Flanges in the rocket exhaust turned, controlled by a gyroscope. They keep the rocket at a steady angle despite changing winds. It was said to be like trying to balance a stick on the back of one's hand, but the A-4 worked.

During World War II, the German dictator Adolf Hitler realized the potential of the rocket. He hoped to use rockets to bomb London and other targets. He ordered General Walter Dornberger to put the weapon in production. The propaganda minister, Joseph Goebbels, renamed the A-4 rocket, calling it the Vengeance Weapon 2, or V-2. The research, development, and manufacture of the weapons during the war was slow and difficult work. The first V-2 rockets were launched only nine months before the defeat of Germany. The Germans fired more than 3,700 V-2s during the last months of the war. Each one carried a one-ton warhead.

Wernher von Braun headed the team of German engineers who moved to the United States after World War II to help develop rockets. He is pictured with a model of a three-stage space rocket he designed while working on missile technology.

Many were aimed at Allied-occupied Antwerp, Belgium. Others landed in London. The weapons could not be precisely aimed, and they often knocked out farmland. Some hit residential areas. Only sometimes did they hit a strategic target like a factory, railroad yard, or bridge.

PRISONERS AND REFUGEES

Many of the people who worked on rocket development in the World War II era were put in prisons. In the Soviet Union, Korolev and Glushko were rounded up by Joseph Stalin's secret police and sent off to labor camps. They joined millions of others, most completely innocent of any crime. The head of the Soviet police, Lavrenti Beria, realized that the

WERNHER VON BRAUN

Wernher Magnus Maximilian von Braun's personal career reflected the typical path of rocket scientists from dreamer-visionaries, through military weapons engineering, to the beginnings of space travel. Born in Wirsitz, Germany (now in Poland), in 1912, he studied in Berlin and in Zurich, Switzerland. In 1930, he joined a group of rocket enthusiasts in Germany, and then was recruited by the German army. The army encouraged von Braun to continue his education. In 1938, he was appointed technical director of a secret facility on the North Sea at Peenemünde. He worked under General Walter Dornberger. There, the two developed the A-4 rocket, later dubbed the V-2.

In March 1944, the Gestapo arrested von Braun. The Gestapo was the German secret police. They accused him of talking too much about space travel. This, they said, sabotaged work on the rocket as a weapon. On the insistence of Dornberger, von Braun was released. Dornberger explained that the V-2 was a first step in the rocket exploration of space.

At the end of World War II, von Braun and most of his senior staff moved westward to surrender to U.S. forces to avoid capture by the Soviet army. His whole team went to Texas. He became the director of the space flight center at Huntsville, Alabama, with 120 members of the original V-2 team. There, von Braun directed work on the Redstone and Jupiter rockets, as well as *Juno II*. The *Juno II* lifted early deep-space probes, *Pioneer III* and *IV*, as well as Explorer satellites. He worked directly for NASA from 1970 to 1972, and he died at age 65 in 1977.

engineers were an important asset, so the best minds were collected and sent to special prison camps known as *sharagas.* There, Beria put them to work designing long-range rockets.

In Germany, prisoners did the manual labor for making the V-2 rockets. Such slave labor staffed the factory at Nordhausen that produced the rockets. Forced labor did much of the construction at Peenemünde on the Baltic Sea. The same SS officers who ran the notorious death camps, such as Auschwitz and Buchenwald, managed the prisoner rocket work. (The SS was a special political police. They served the Nazi party. The SS ran the death camps. They also murdered people who stood against the Nazis.)

World War II ended in 1945. Both the United States and the Soviet Union wanted to learn how to make V-2 rockets, so they offered German engineers pay and interesting work. Most of the engineers took the new jobs. If they had stayed in Germany, none of them would have been able to continue working in the rocket business. Both the United States and the Soviet Union were able, within a short span of a decade, to build new generations of rockets. They applied the V-2 principles to build new rockets, which were able to reach the fringes of outer space.

UNITED STATES: ROBERT GODDARD AND OTHERS

Earlier, through the 1920s and 1930s, Americans had also worked on liquid-fueled rockets, however, they did not have much support from the government. The key researcher in the United States was Robert Goddard (1882–1945). As a teenager, in 1899, he read the novel *War of the Worlds* by H. G. Wells, in which Martians invaded Earth. Goddard studied physics and attended Clark University, where he earned a doctorate studying under Nobel Prize winner Albert Michelson. Goddard won a research grant from the Smithsonian Institution and produced a short pamphlet in 1920 entitled *A Method of Reaching Extreme Altitudes.* In this 69-page booklet, he calculated the escape velocity and thrust needed to lift a rocket off the surface of Earth. He also calculated that it could be crashed into the Moon. The idea caught the imagination of newspaper writers. Goddard was soon popularized as the "Moon Man" in newspapers across the United States.

Goddard was shy and the publicity shocked him. He became more withdrawn but continued to work on rocket projects. He developed a liquid-fueled rocket in 1926—before the similar German and Soviet projects—but his first rocket flew less than 200 feet (60.9 m). As a physicist, he was not a great mechanic and he tended to work alone, often on small models to test out principles.

Even so, his ideas attracted interest. One day in 1929, he got a phone call from Charles Lindbergh. Lindbergh was internationally famous for his solo trans-Atlantic flight in 1927. Lindbergh listened to Goddard's ideas and helped him arrange a grant from the Guggenheim Foundation. The money was enough for Goddard to move to New Mexico and set up a small laboratory of his own together with a test facility outside Roswell. He kept working on rockets and getting patents on gyroscopic controls and other aspects of the system. The patent documents were available to the public. In Germany, von Braun collected copies of the U.S. patents, which included detailed drawings and explanations. Von Braun admitted later that some of the ideas for the A-series and V-2 rockets were taken from Goddard's patents.

As a loner, Goddard stayed away from other rocket scientists. Editors and writers of the science fiction magazine *Science Wonder Stories* formed a group in New York. They set up an organization called the American Interplanetary Society. Soon they changed the name to the American Rocket Society (ARS). As was the case for similar groups in Moscow and Berlin, the club lacked funds; however, it had many enthusiastic members who dreamed of space travel. The ARS arranged a showing of Lang's *Girl in the Moon,* attracting a huge audience and gaining a few new members.

With a small budget and borrowed tools, the group arranged rocket tests on Staten Island, New York. Later they moved to a more open space in New Jersey. Their work attracted James Wyld (1913–1953), who had begun building rockets after finishing his degree at Princeton. Wyld and another ARS member, Lovell Lawrence (1915–1971), were able to convince the U.S. Navy to support their work, but only if the two would form a company. The two men set up Reaction Motors, Incorporated, and began to work on navy contracts. The company later merged with Thiokol Chemical Corporation.

Robert Goddard patented several techniques and devices for stabilizing liquid-fueled rockets in flight. Although he never built large rockets, his ideas anticipated many of the details later used in the German V-2 rockets built by Wernher von Braun. Here, Goddard stands beside the launch platform minutes before this small rocket made one of the first successful flights by a liquid-fueled rocket in 1926.

During World War II, American rocketry began to expand. Goddard went to the Annapolis Marine Engineering Laboratory. There he worked under Robert Truax on jet-assisted takeoff, or JATO, rockets. A few months before his death from cancer in 1945, Goddard inspected a captured V-2 rocket. He studied it closely. A colleague asked if the V-2 parts resembled Goddard's own ideas. Quietly, Goddard admitted, they did.

At the California Institute of Technology (Caltech), a professor of aeronautic engineering, Theodor von Kármán (1881–1963), collected a group of scientists to work on rockets. They began testing rockets in nearby hills. As the California academics began work on war projects, they formed a special unit of the institute, the Jet Propulsion Laboratory, to take on defense research work. Some of them later went on to form the company Aerojet General.

FOLLOWING UP ON THE V-2

When the war ended, both the Soviet Union and the United States tried to round up parts and complete V-2 rockets, together with the scientists, engineers, and technicians who had worked on them. The United States was able to bring back, across the Atlantic, numerous complete rockets and most of the top technical people. The Soviets established contact with one or two factories that had made components, as well as many of the lower-level technicians. So, in 1945, both countries began to build directly on the V-2 experience.

In the United States, von Braun and some 120 others from his Peenemünde group began testing and demonstrating V-2 rockets at White Sands, New Mexico, not far from where the United States had tested its first nuclear weapon in July 1945. In 1946–1947, several projects went forward at the same time, with funding from different branches of the U.S. military. Later, von Braun and his group moved to Huntsville, Alabama, and worked at the Redstone Arsenal there.

Meanwhile, engineers made several new U.S. rockets. The Jet Propulsion Laboratory developed the WAC Corporal in 1947 for the U.S. Army, with an engine built by Reaction Motors. By 1949, a WAC Corporal rocket reached a height of 244 miles (392 km), a record held until 1956. The navy paid for studies that led to a successful flight of the Viking rocket in 1954. The Viking took one of the first pictures of Earth from outer space, showing the curvature out over the Pacific Ocean. The U.S. Air Force contracted with North American Aviation, which hired some of von Braun's staff. Building on the V-2 experience, they designed a winged rocket known as the Navaho. The Navaho engines produced 75,000 pounds (34,019 kilograms) of thrust compared to the V-2's 56,000 pounds (25,401 kg).

ATOMIC WEAPONS

The first atomic bombs were developed in a secret program known as the Manhattan Project. They were far more powerful than any weapon ever seen before. The United States tested its first bomb in July 1945 at a site in New Mexico. Then, less than a month later, two atomic bombs were dropped on Japan. The first devastated Hiroshima on August 6, 1945. The second fell on Nagasaki on August 8, 1945. The two weapons killed about 300,000 people, mostly civilians. Soon after the bombings, the Japanese surrendered on August 15. They formally signed the surrender documents on September 2, 1945, that ended World War II.

The United States now had nuclear weapons. It also had long-range aircraft capable of reaching many cities in the Soviet Union. Stalin ordered his scientists, led by Igor Kurchatov, to develop an atomic bomb. They followed the American design, which had been obtained through spies. Stalin also ordered Sergei Korolev and Valentin Glushko to improve on the V-2. They were the Soviet Union's leading rocket designers. Stalin wanted a rocket that could carry a nuclear weapon from the Soviet Union to the United States. This began the arms race between the Soviet Union and the United States, which lasted for decades. Much of the arms race was conducted in secret. The "cold war" between the two nations began in 1948.

A year later, in August 1949, the Soviet Union tested its first atomic bomb. It was known as "Joe 1" after Joseph Stalin. Soon, the British and Americans learned that the Manhattan Project had been penetrated by spies. One spy in particular, Klaus Fuchs, admitted to spying for the Soviets. He had given his Russian spymasters detailed drawings and specially written reports. The work of Fuchs and other spies allowed the Soviet program to move quickly forward to its first bomb.

The Soviet Union lacked long-range bombers, while American bombers, based in Western Europe, could easily strike Soviet cities.

The threat of a retaliation attack, American military planners believed, would prevent any aggressive Soviet action since American response would lead to destruction of Soviet cities. Even so, the United States went ahead to develop a more powerful thermonuclear weapon—the hydrogen bomb, or H-bomb. It was incredibly destructive; it could destroy a city and its surrounding region. Meanwhile, the Soviet Union also developed a similar weapon, testing it within about a year of the first American test.

COLD WAR AND MISSILE ACHIEVEMENTS

In the face of such horrible weapons of mass destruction, the cold war intensified. The two nations and their allies worried that any small crisis could grow into a full-fledged war. Yet many military strategists in the United States believed during the 1950s that the Soviet Union was far behind in rocket development. After all, many of the leading German rocket designers had come to the United States after World War II.

During the International Geophysical Year from July 1957 to December 1958, the United States anticipated launching a satellite. However, the Soviet Union won the race to launch a satellite successfully. The Soviets put the satellite *Sputnik 1* in orbit around Earth on October 4, 1957. The team, headed by Korolev, worked from a well-financed cosmodrome in the Soviet republic of Kazakhstan.

Around the world, teams of volunteers had been set up to track satellites. The Soviets installed aboard *Sputnik* a radio beacon broadcasting on ham radio frequencies. The broadcasts made radio tracking a lot easier. A month after *Sputnik 1,* on November 3, 1957, the Soviets launched *Sputnik 2.* Aboard was a dog named Laika.

The Soviets were also quietly working on military rockets. Stalin wanted to meet the threat posed by the U.S. bomber aircraft. His rocket engineers designed a rocket capable of carrying a heavy nuclear weapon all the way to the United States. Korolev led the construction of the R-7 rocket. It was powered with a cluster of 20 liquid-oxygen-and-kerosene-fueled engines. The R-7 met Stalin's need for an intercontinental ballistic missile, or ICBM rocket. The R-7 could also launch satellites.

Sputnik 1 initiated the "space race" between the Soviet Union and the United States. A Jupiter booster lifted the first U.S. satellite,

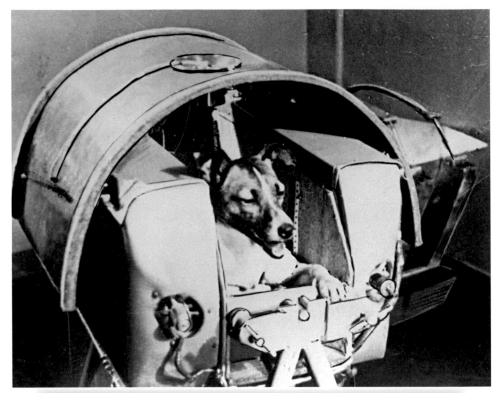

On November 3,1957, Laika became the first living creature ever sent to space, onboard *Sputnik II*. Laika died a few hours after launch from stress and overheating, likely due to a malfunction of the thermal control system.

Explorer 1, into orbit on January 31, 1958. The first successful Vanguard series launch was March 17, 1958. Exploration of space by rocket—born out of military competition but inspired by a generation of amateurs and dreamers—had begun.

THE MISSILE GAP

By 1958, Americans began to fear the Soviet Union had gotten ahead in the arms race. New programs funded higher education, and money for research flowed out of Washington, D.C. Politicians talked of a possible "missile gap." This meant that the United States had fallen behind in missile development, and the Soviets had pulled ahead. To the Soviet leaders, it was more important that the Americans and their allies believe the Soviets were ahead, than it was to be actually ahead.

By boasting about their missile strength, the Soviets fed the idea that there was a missile gap. By 1960, polls showed throughout the Western countries that people believed the Soviets were ahead of the United States in military strength. They also believed that their lead would grow in the future. The Soviets kept much of their program secret. No one outside the country knew the location of the launch sites, the names of the scientists involved, and the amounts of money spent. All of the secrecy fed anxiety among Europeans and Americans.

Meanwhile, the Soviet preparations for manned space travel went forward. In 1958, Korolev converted an obsolete aircraft factory near Moscow into a "manned space flight center." The Americans began their own manned program known as Project Mercury in 1958. The Soviet program was known as Vostok, meaning "the east." The name suggested that the progress of the human race came from the Soviets, not from the West.

COSMONAUT VS. ASTRONAUT: THE RACE FOR SPACE

The Soviets called their spacecraft pilots "cosmonauts." The Americans planned to put "astronauts" in space. By 1958, an offshoot of the cold war and the arms race became the race to put a cosmonaut or astronaut in space first.

The two nations' plans were slightly different. The Soviet Vostok plan was to send a man aloft and have him orbit Earth. He would then drop through the atmosphere in a capsule and parachute to the ground with a personal harness parachute. The American Mercury plan was to shoot a man into space on a rocket in a long arc. He would return to Earth in a parachute-slowed capsule about 300 miles (482 km) from the launch site. Americans hoped launching the first "man in space" might help in the propaganda war with the Soviet Union. While not an orbit, it would still count as putting a man in space and bringing him home safely.

Through 1959–1961, both countries had some failures in their projects. The U.S. Army had developed a long-range Jupiter rocket, and it was used to carry two monkeys, named Able and Baker, into near space in May 1959. The Redstone rocket held out promise for a longer flight, and was joined to a Mercury capsule capable of carrying a man.

However, the test shot in November 1960 failed. The Mercury-Redstone match-up was known as the MR series. On December 19, 1960, the empty MR-1A did all right. It reached an altitude of 131 miles (210 km). MR-2 went up on January 31, 1961, carrying a chimpanzee named Ham. Ham survived the flight, despite a few mistakes. He had to wait over two hours after landing in the ocean some 130 miles (209 km) beyond the target zone, bobbing around in the Atlantic Ocean before rescuers arrived.

Seven human astronauts stood ready to go into space on the first available MR. Concerned with safety, NASA engineers decided to test the MR system one more time. On March 24, 1961, another MR without anyone aboard flew successfully. It splashed down right on target.

Meanwhile, Korolev worked with the Vostok team. The Soviet scientists kept close tabs on the highly publicized American program. On April 12, 1961, Korolev fired up a modified ICBM. Yuri Alekseyevich Gagarin was aboard. Gagarin completed one orbit around the world in 90 minutes. He landed by parachute in a pasture in central Russia. Thus the Russians won the race to put the first human in space.

American specialists were disappointed. Navy commander Alan Bartlett Shepard had been ready and willing to go into his suborbital flight in March, several weeks before Gagarin. The empty test MR vehicle could have carried him. Instead, he flew on May 5, 1961, in a tiny spacecraft named *Freedom 7*. Launched from Cape Canaveral, Florida, Shepard reached an altitude of 115 miles (185 km). A few days later, President John Kennedy presented Shepard with a Distinguished Service Medal. Kennedy was impressed with Shepard and excited by the whole space competition. The fact that Gagarin got to space a few weeks earlier than Shepard would only spur further competition. As the first men in space, Gagarin and Shepard became heroes in their home countries. They also became symbols for the competition between the two nations.

Only much later did news leak about a major accident in the Soviet space program, much worse than any of the minor setbacks that had troubled the Americans. Under Premier Nikita Khrushchev, the Soviets had hoped to score an even bigger success that would impress the world in 1960. They had planned to send an unmanned rocket to Mars in October 1960, timed to be announced when Khrushchev visited the United Nations in New York City, but two rockets fizzled out after leaving their launchpads on October 10 and 14. Then on October 23, a third rocket failed to ignite. The technicians were ordered out of their protective blockhouses to examine the rocket. As they approached, the propellants in the rocket exploded, killing many of the engineers and technicians. The exact number was never released.

The technical side of the race was another story. The Russian equipment was poorly designed. Soviet rocketry had been a force-fed development in a military economy. It depended on shifting resources away from other important areas. Progress in rocketry really came at a price that held back the progress of the Soviet nation.

For American president John F. Kennedy, the competition had become a burning issue. He was already contemplating the next step in the international space race: a mission to the Moon.

4

The Race
for the Moon

On May 25, 1961, President John F. Kennedy, in a speech to a joint session of Congress, posed a dramatic challenge to the nation. He proposed that the United States

> *should commit itself to achieving the goal, before this decade is out, of landing a man on the moon and returning him safely to [E]arth. No single space project in this period will be more impressive to mankind, or more important for the long-range exploration of space; and none will be so difficult or expensive to accomplish.*

Why did he make this astounding statement? The reasons are linked to the nature of the Kennedy presidency. Kennedy, at age 43, had campaigned against the administration of Dwight Eisenhower, representing his own team as a new generation willing to take on new frontiers. Kennedy sought to challenge the Soviet Union for a position of leadership among the nations of the world. The recent victory of the Soviets in placing Yuri Gagarin in space three weeks before NASA astronaut Alan Shepard was the final nudge to action. Kennedy's motives were summed up in his speech. He wanted both to be "impressive to mankind" and to advance the "long-range exploration of space."

Over the next eight and a half years, NASA pushed an expensive and risky program. In order to meet the goal, NASA had to navigate two very difficult dilemmas. One was technical; the other was political.

Accompanied by Vice President Lyndon B. Johnson (*right*) and Wernher von Braun (*second, right*), President John F. Kennedy (*front*) inspects a display of the Saturn C-1 booster rocket at the Marshall Space Center.

THE TECHNICAL DILEMMA

Engineers faced the pressure of an impossible schedule. The goal was clear: They needed to reach the Moon "before this decade is out." The round trip had to be made before December 31, 1969. That meant that NASA had to pressure designers to come up with workable machines and to constantly press contractors to provide solutions to problems. However, they could not take extra time while developing the solutions. The disaster on *Apollo 13* was one crisis faced by the program. Yet it was by no means the only or the worst one.

Accidents revealed technical mistakes that seemed obvious when looking back. They were overlooked in the rush to meet the schedule. NASA knew it could not be too concerned with perfection. Seeking perfection would lead to a "failure" to meet the deadline. On the other hand, rushing to meet the schedule could lead to deadly accidents. By taking on some risks, and aiming at systems that performed well and staffing them with brilliant pilots and scientists, NASA found its way. Tragic losses were taken in stride, and shots to the Moon went off with less-than-perfect equipment. After all, the machines usually could be made to work. They could accomplish some, if not all, of the expected objectives.

THE POLITICAL DILEMMA

Another dilemma concerned publicity. NASA needed public and political support. It surrounded astronauts with reporters, hoping to make the astronauts heroes in the eyes of the public. The public attention showered on the astronauts proved that the public recognized their bravery. At the same time, the publicity was often a distraction from their real work. Whenever an accident happened, the public attention on the men and their families could backfire and bring with it, perhaps, the loss of public support. So NASA walked a public affairs tightrope through the decade, trying to woo the support of the media and always fearing that slippage of schedule or human tragedy could destroy that support.

NASA encouraged the media to make heroes out of the astronauts. In 1966 alone, astronauts made 810 public appearances. They gave 314 formal presentations. The public affairs office handled another 1,600 appearance requests and processed more than 70,000 letters. The astronauts liked the perks that came with the job, such as the loan of Corvette sports cars by a Florida auto dealer. They got special discounts at a luxury resort in Acapulco. Some received regular payments from *Life* magazine for articles they wrote. Still, they often resented the limelight. Sometimes they threatened to limp or to mark their faces with dye to simulate illness if the public affairs office would not hold back the flood of cameras.

UNDERLYING REASONS FOR THE RACE

As Kennedy's vice president, Lyndon Johnson headed the Space Council. In a report to the president before Kennedy's May speech, Johnson listed six reasons why the Moon venture should be undertaken. The reasons showed how the goal was an extension of the cold war competition with the Soviet Union.

1. The Soviet Union was ahead in prestige.
2. The United States had so far failed to bring its own superior technical resources to bear on space.
3. Other countries would line up with the country that seemed to be the leader.
4. If the United States failed to take action, the Soviets would extend their lead so far that the United States would not be able to catch up.
5. Even in areas where the Soviets were ahead, the United States should make aggressive efforts.
6. Manned exploration of the Moon was of great propaganda value and was also essential to the advancement of human knowledge.

One delicate issue was the question of the military value of the enterprise. An overemphasis on the military benefits of the space program could result in a falloff in world opinion and support. Thus the effort was mounted through NASA, the new civilian agency that had been formed in 1958, rather than through the U.S. Air Force.

To ensure the peaceful program, as defined by the United States, President Johnson signed the international Outer Space Treaty, ratified by the U.S. Senate on February 7, 1967. The treaty declared that there would be no national sovereignty over space (just as there was no national sovereignty over the open oceans). The treaty banned the placement of weapons in outer space. At the same time, it did not forbid satellites designed to gather military intelligence, did not require that other countries cooperate in space ventures, and did not forbid the use of military personnel or even military equipment (such as the rockets themselves) in space exploration. Under the treaty, the United States could work out agreements with Australia and Kenya to set up tracking stations to monitor its space vehicles, but such countries would not be required to offer similar facilities to the Soviets.

THE GEMINI FLIGHTS

The Gemini series of space flights were held between 1964 and 1966. They were two-man flights intended to test navigation and space maneuvers needed for later missions. These included techniques such as docking in space and controlling the flight of a spacecraft to maneuver it into position. The Gemini astronauts also practiced extravehicular activity (EVA), also known as spacewalking. Altogether there were

The U.S. Navy assist the *Gemini 6* astronauts, Thomas Stafford (*left*) and Wally Schirra, as they emerge from the reentry capsule after splashdown on their return from a space mission.

12 Gemini missions. The first two missions, which were unmanned, proved that the heat shield worked on reentry and tested the performance of systems and subsystems, ground control, and guidance. They also provided important training for the ground controllers.

There were serious technical problems on nearly every Gemini mission. In many cases, the returning capsule missed the target area of the ocean. Some activities and maneuvers were canceled because of excessive fuel consumption or faulty equipment. Two of the missions, *Gemini* 6 and 9, had to be rescheduled because the liftoff rockets failed. Illnesses, heart conditions, and the accidental death of two astronauts (Elliot See and Charles Bassett) during training meant a constantly changing schedule of assignments.

The astronauts pointed out that they had to be able to react to challenges when the missions did not go as predicted. So from the first, the astronauts argued that they were pilots, not just poster boys for NASA. The Original Seven and the New Nine were all qualified and trained as pilots. All had come to the space program from military careers.

APOLLO PROJECTS

The three-man Apollo projects began in 1967 and continued through 1971. After six unmanned flights, the first manned shot, *Apollo 7*, was launched on October 11, 1968, to test the spacecraft in Earth's orbit.

Apollo 7 had been delayed because of a tragic accident in January 1967. Three astronauts were killed in a fire in an Apollo capsule (*AS-204*) during a test on the ground. Virgil (Gus) Grissom, Edward White, and Roger Chaffee were testing the Apollo craft on the ground. They were wearing their space suits and breathing a pure oxygen atmosphere. The fire started with bad wiring under one of the astronaut's couches; the oxygen fed the fire. As the fire burned, pressure built up inside. The craft's door was designed to open inward, and the pressure held it closed. The astronauts could not open it. It was several minutes before ground crews arrived to try to free the victims. By then they had suffocated from the poisonous gases released during the intense fire.

The disaster became the subject of much controversy. Critics blamed NASA for not heeding warnings about the dangers of a pure oxygen atmosphere. The failure of the door, the slow response of rescue teams, the lack of firefighting equipment, and the decision by

THE ORIGINAL SEVEN AND NEW NINE

The first NASA astronauts were recruited in groups, and soon the press caught on to the names given to the different groups. The Original Seven had flown in Mercury missions. Many of the New Nine flew on Apollo missions. Other classes of astronauts were in groups of 14 and 19. In all, there were about 50 astronauts in NASA's program between 1962 and 1971. The early astronauts became so well known that the press and American public usually remembered them by their nicknames.

The Original Seven (1959)	The New Nine (1962)
Scott Carpenter	Neil Armstrong
Gordo Cooper	Frank Borman
John Glenn	Charles Conrad
Gus Grissom	Jim Lovell
Wally Schirra	Jim McDivitt
Alan Shepard	Elliott See
Deke Slayton	Thomas Stafford
	Edward White
	John Young

NASA to investigate its own accident, all caused negative reactions. Nevertheless, the media generally remained supportive. The tragic deaths were mourned, and the program went ahead. NASA continued struggling to meet the deadline of a man on the Moon by the end of the 1960s.

APOLLO 11: A DREAM FULFILLED

The most memorable of the flights was the first to land on the Moon, *Apollo 11,* in July 1969. The trip not only fulfilled President Kennedy's challenge, it also captured the imagination of the world.

Apollo 11 was a three-part spacecraft. It had a lunar module (LM), command module, and service module. When the craft reached an orbit around the Moon, the LM would separate from the joined command and service modules. Astronaut Michael Collins would remain aboard the command module, while Neil Armstrong and Edwin (Buzz) Aldrin descended in the LM to get out and walk on the surface of the Moon. Altogether there were six successful lunar landings.

On July 20, 1969, the world watched as the two astronauts experimented with walking in the reduced lunar gravity. Knowing that a major historical event was about to take place, Armstrong prepared himself with a memorable line. Yet stepping down out of the lunar lander took considerable preparation. Six hours and 21 minutes after landing, Armstrong and Aldrin pulled open the hatch. Aldrin watched as Armstrong slowly backed out of the lander, moving his bulky backpack carefully from side to side. He then lowered himself to one of the landing pads that were like feet on the lander.

He checked to make sure he could step back up from the landing pad to the first rung on the ladder. Then he stepped off onto the surface of the Moon. A television camera aboard the ship transmitted his image as he said, "That's one small step for man, one giant leap for mankind." Soon Aldrin came out. Armstrong noted that the surface was "fine and powdery" and that he could pick it up loosely with the toe of his boot. Aldrin remarked at the view: "magnificent desolation." Together the two astronauts planted a plaque that read: "Here Man from the planet Earth first set foot upon the Moon, July 1969 A.D. We came in peace for all mankind." Aldrin and Armstrong then raised an American flag, on a pole that did not quite stick properly in the hard surface.

Michael Collins circled in the command module above the surface of the Moon. He heard from flight control that the flag had been set. He noted dryly that he was probably the only person in the universe who was not watching the event on television.

The shots of their footprints in the dust of the Moon and their attempts to develop kangaroo hops were avidly watched everywhere on Earth where there were television receivers. Armstrong and Aldrin gathered some samples of rock, and after nearly a day on the surface, they lifted off the surface for a safe mating with the command module and a return to a heroes' welcome on Earth.

On July 20, 1969, the *Apollo 11* astronauts Neil Armstrong and Buzz Aldrin (*pictured*) made history when they became the first men to walk on the Moon. They planted a plaque, then raised and saluted the American flag.

The fire on *AS-204* and the near-disaster of the *Apollo 13* mission did not stop the completion of the remaining missions. Many astronauts waited their turn for a chance to continue Moon exploration. They were disappointed when NASA decided to cancel moon-landing missions *Apollo 18, 19,* and *20.*

Why did NASA cancel the last trips? Despite the six successful returns of astronauts from the Moon, public interest had declined. Having fulfilled Kennedy's goal, it was difficult to justify continuing the mission for solely scientific results. As outlined by Vice President Johnson in early 1961, the mission had been quite clear: Beat the Soviet Union to the Moon. The always-secondary scientific side no longer seemed worth the expenditure of billions of dollars.

THE MOON IN THE 1960s

The success of the Moon mission achieved its purpose. In the early 1960s, popular opinion was that the United States was "behind" the Soviets in the space race. That notion was gone by the end of 1969.

There were other consequences of the Moon race. The success of Project Apollo proved that problems could be addressed by a combined national effort. Americans often referred to this achievement when they faced challenges in future decades. "If we can land a man on the moon, why can't we . . .?" (finishing with such ideas as "end poverty," "find a cure for cancer," or "clean up the environment"). Of course, many problems were not as easily addressed by technology and money. Still, Kennedy's challenge represented a can-do attitude.

An important by-product of the Moon race was the Outer Space Treaty signed in 1967. The treaty reduced the arms incentive for space exploration and made the focus of space exploration truly scientific. Many saw the Moon trip as a great step in the long adventure of human-kind's exploration. The landing of *Apollo 11* on July 18, 1969, was viewed by many as the beginning of the space age. Outer space may have been already conquered with astronauts in orbit and on the surface of the Moon, but the mysteries of the universe continued to lure the human race to further exploration. In the next decades, space exploration focused on a step-by-step gathering of information by a wide variety of means.

Even as the race for the Moon was in progress, planners and engineers in the Soviet Union and the United States anticipated the next steps in the exploration of space. They imagined orbiting space stations, robotic trips to other planets, and improved observation from Earth. They hoped to continue to further push back the frontier.

5

Space Stations

Dreamers such as Wernher von Braun and Robert Goddard had visualized the day when rockets would carry humans into outer space. They and hundreds of science fiction authors writing in the 1940s and 1950s believed that by the end of the twentieth century human beings would have permanent settlements off planet Earth. Their expectations turned out to be almost right. The United States put *Skylab* in orbit in 1973. On this space station small groups of astronauts could be in space for more than 100 days each, during which several shifts of crews gathered valuable information. In 1986, the Soviets placed *Mir* in orbit, sending up a total of five modules that were linked together into a true space station. After 15 years of service and several near-disasters, the *Mir* was brought down in a fiery descent into the Pacific Ocean in 2001. More permanent was the *International Space Station*. It was assembled over a period of seven years, 1998–2004, and supported by a dozen nations. By the early twenty-first century, there was indeed a near-permanent presence of the human race living off the planet Earth.

SKYLAB

Skylab was launched May 14, 1973. Its goal was to learn exactly how humans could live in space for a long period of time. The *Gemini 7* crew of Frank Borman and Jim Lovell had stayed in space for almost two weeks. A Russian team aboard *Soyuz 9* was in orbit for 18 days, however, medical experts worried that long periods of weightlessness might

Skylab, the United States' first space station, was designed to house humans in space for an extended period of time. Ground training included learning every detail of the mechanical systems and testing the astronauts' ability to maintain their sense of orientation in the weightless environment. Above, astronauts practice working on the *Skylab* while weightless underwater at the training facility in Huntsville, Alabama.

cause permanent physical damage. Scientists also wondered about the psychological effects of weightlessness and confinement in space. *Skylab* would provide an opportunity to study those questions.

The original idea for *Skylab* was to orbit an empty rocket fuel tank that would then be equipped with areas for living, communication, and a workshop-laboratory. However, as plans developed and the difficulty of construction in space was better understood, NASA decided to equip *Skylab* on the ground. It would send it into space ready to receive humans.

Skylab had outside dimensions of about 48 feet by about 22 feet (14 m by 6 m). It had living and working space of about 1,100 cubic feet

(335 cubic m). A crew of three would live, work, eat, sleep, and use the bathroom in an area about the size of a camping trailer. Power was provided by solar arrays while they were in the sunlit period of the orbit. Rotating the laboratory through the sunlight and into shade provided heating and cooling. The air inside the craft could be circulated and purified.

Three separate manned missions were scheduled, totaling 171 days in space over a period of nine months. The crews would have to make their own repairs as unexpected problems developed. Thus, the crews learned every detail of *Skylab's* mechanical systems. They became experts in the tools, spares, filters, waste equipment, and assorted backup hardware. Procedures were worked out for more than 150 different repair tasks, and the crew practiced all of them. The first mission involved lots of repair work to *Skylab*, which was damaged on takeoff.

Each of the three crews had a backup crew. Many of the astronauts in training had never been in space before. However, Charles Conrad had flown on *Gemini 5* and *Gemini 11*. He had walked on the Moon on *Apollo 12*. So Conrad was chosen to head the first *Skylab* crew. Alan Bean had been the lunar module pilot on *Apollo 12*. He headed the second team. The *Skylab* missions provided vast quantities of data on the problems of living in a weightless environment. They laid the groundwork for longer stays in space aboard future space stations.

MIR

The Soviet Union also planned to regularly lift crews from Earth and take them to orbiting satellites. The Soviets hoped to conduct observations, build their own living and working spaces, and begin programs of regular scientific work. They used their large rockets to launch Salyut capsules, containing astronauts and equipment.

In 1986, the Soviets built a more permanent space station, known as the *Mir*. *Mir* remained in operation for 15 years. Leonid Kizim and Vladimir Solovyov were the first *Mir* crew. They were ferried aboard a *Soyuz* spacecraft to *Salyut 7* and opened the station. They lived there for almost two months. In March 1987, a second module, known as *Kvant 1*, arrived at the *Mir* station. However, a problem developed. The hatches between the two modules could not be opened. Members of the crew, in an unscheduled space walk, found that a prior visit by a Progress cargo ship had left a bag of trash that jammed the hatch opening.

Numerous astronauts from other nations visited *Mir* for short stays. These included crewmembers from France, Syria, and Afghanistan. Later, Toyohiro Akiyama, as a Japanese "space correspondent," visited the *Mir* station, broadcasting live for a Tokyo television station. In 1989, the *Kvant 2* module was attached. In 1990, cosmonauts Alexander Serebrov and Alexander Victorenko rode in "flying armchairs" more than 100 feet (30 m) from the station, tied to the station by long leads.

Simply supplying and occupying the station required several on-the-job adjustments and temporary fixes. During a space walk in 1990, cosmonauts repaired a thermal layer on the *Soyuz* spacecraft that was used to shuttle crews up to the *Mir* and back to Earth. They had never been trained to make the repair, yet they pulled it off successfully. As they returned to *Mir*, they damaged an airlock and had to go back into *Mir* by way of a compartment in the *Kvant 2* module.

After the break up of the Soviet Union in 1991, *Mir* received crews that included astronauts from Austria and from the former Soviet republic of Kazakhstan. Later visits included astronauts from Germany and France. Several records were set by the crews aboard *Mir*. Valeri Polyakov had the longest stay in space—438 days.

The U.S. space shuttle *Atlantis* docked with *Mir* in 1995. Norman Thagard, an American astronaut, conducted experiments there for several months. Several other Americans spent various periods up to a few months aboard the *Mir*. In 1996, American astronaut Shannon Lucid spent almost six months onboard. She set the record for the longest stay by an American astronaut in space up to that time.

In 1997, the station suffered some of its worst accidents. In February, a lithium candle started a fire. When burned, these candles give off oxygen. It took the crew more than an hour to extinguish the fire. Flames behave very differently in a weightless environment. The fire could easily have killed the whole crew and destroyed the station. Later, in June, a Progress cargo craft veered off course and banged into the station a number of times. One of the *Mir* modules was punctured and started to lose pressure. Working quickly, the crew managed to seal off the damaged compartment before the pressure inside the main part of the *Mir* station fell too low. After several more international visits to the now damaged and dirty station, the last crew left *Mir* in 1999.

An American businessman began to train astronauts to repair *Mir*. He hoped to send tourists up to it; however, that plan and others to make profits from *Mir* all fell through. The Russian space agency decided to bring *Mir* down. The "deorbiting" was a bit risky because *Mir*, which weighed 135 tons, was the largest human-made object ever to be aimed down at Earth from outer space. The earlier descent of the 40-ton space station *Salyut 7* in 1991 went off course and crashed into South America. Fortunately, it hit an unpopulated region. The much larger and heavier *Mir* had five separate linked modules that were predicted to break apart upon reentry. When the Progress rockets fired, it forced the *Mir* into the proper planned landing in the Pacific. Observers on the Fiji Islands were treated to a spectacular fireworks display as the giant pieces of the station glowed as they melted from the atmosphere's friction.

Although the *Mir* station was not equipped for much scientific work, it did provide a laboratory where the effects of living and working in space could be studied. Cosmonauts and astronauts learned how to cooperate in making EVAs, or space walks. Altogether, astronauts and cosmonauts from 10 different countries spent time gathering great amounts of data about life in space.

SHUTTLE-*MIR* PROGRAM

Over a 27-month period from 1996 to 1998, teams of American astronauts lived and worked aboard *Mir* at various periods. They prepared for the assembly and operation of the *International Space Station* (*ISS*). The goal of the Shuttle-*Mir* Program was to gain experience in Russian-American cooperation and practices.

The astronauts on *Mir* looked for ways to reduce the construction costs and risks for the *ISS* by testing out different designs and procedures. They gained experience on long missions and conducted experiments. They discovered that living in microgravity causes a 1.2 percent loss of bone mass in the lower hip and spine per month. Other experiments showed that plants could be grown and the seeds could be harvested, proving that it was possible to grow plants for food in outer space.

INTERNATIONAL SPACE STATION (ISS)

The first parts of the *International Space Station (ISS)* were lifted into space in 1998. Construction continued into 2004. Parts of the *ISS* were provided by the United States, Russia, Canada, Brazil, and Japan. Parts were also provided by 10 member countries of the European Space Agency (ESA): Belgium, Denmark, France, Germany, Italy, the Netherlands, Norway, Spain, Sweden, and Switzerland. Both the Americans and the Russians drew on their prior experiences, with *Skylab* and with *Mir*, to plan and assemble the *ISS*.

The cooperation between Russia and the United States was extensive. The Russians launched their components and crews, which sometimes included Americans or people of other nationalities, from the Baikonur Cosmodrome in Kazakhstan. The Americans delivered parts by space shuttles launched from Cape Canaveral, in Florida. The Russians put the first module in space. Known as *Zarya* (sunrise), it was launched in November 1998. The *Unity* module soon followed, taken up on U.S. shuttle voyage STS-88. Regular flights by both nations brought up supplies through 1999 and 2000. The Russians attached the *Zvezda* (star) service module in July 2000. Shuttle missions by *Discovery* and *Atlantis* took up supplies, batteries, and equipment for the living compartments. Crews began living aboard in November 2000. A laboratory was attached in January 2001, and the crews were exchanged the following month. The Canada Arm, a long boom that allowed spacewalking astronauts to have a stable platform while working outside the station, was added in 2001. Italy and Japan provided other modules.

When completed, the *ISS* had a 365-foot (111-m) wingspan. It houses up to seven people and contains six separate laboratories. It weighs one million pounds (453,592 kg), three times the weight of *Mir*. The *ISS* rotates 220 miles (354 km) above Earth. It allows humans to explore in space 24 hours a day, 7 days a week, 365 days a year. It is humankind's first permanent off-Earth living facility.

INTERNATIONAL EFFORT

Cooperation in space between the Soviet Union and the United States had begun in the 1970s; however, the *ISS* represented a truly international effort. In addition to the Russian-American cooperation, many

Construction of the *International Space Station* (*ISS*) began in 1998, and is scheduled for completion in 2011. A joint project between the space agencies of many nations, the space station (which can be seen from Earth with the naked eye) has been continuously staffed since November 2000.

other countries participated with crucial parts of the final station. Canada provided the Space Station Remote Manipulator System, which was an improvement over the original mechanical arm designed and built in Canada. Canada also developed the robotic Canada Hand, or Special Purpose Dexterous Manipulator. The ESA built a pressurized laboratory, launched on a French rocket. Japan provided an exterior platform for experiments and also logistics transport vehicles. Russia provided two research modules as well as the station's living quarters. In addition, the Russians regularly supplied the *ISS* with their transport vehicles launched from Baikonur. Other pieces of equipment came from Brazil and Italy, including a pallet to house external payloads and an Earth observation facility.

The object of the *ISS* was not simply to show that all of these nations could get along. It was also not just to prove that humans could live and work for long periods in space. Rather, the nations hoped to build a permanent laboratory in space in order to conduct a wide variety of practical experiments. Researchers planned protein crystal studies and examinations of tissue culture. They sought to learn how low gravity would affect humans, plants, insects, and other life forms. They would study the characteristics of flames, fluids, and molten metal in space. Others planned experiments in physics and the nature of space.

The *ISS* provides an ideal platform for observation of Earth. It also provides opportunities not possible on Earth. New types of pharmaceuticals and microscopic technologies (known as nanotechnology) might be best made in a gravity-free environment.

This period in space exploration was not all positive, however. Critics on Earth pointed to the tragedies that had accompanied space travel. Two of the worst tragedies occurred with American shuttle crafts.

6

The Space Shuttles

AFTER PROJECT APOLLO, NASA TRIED TO SHOW THE PRACTICAL results that could come from space exploration. *Skylab* proved that funding could be found for a research program in outer space. Engineers worked on designs for reusable, rather than expendable, crafts. They were called space shuttles.

THE SHUTTLE FLEET

The space shuttle, also known as an orbiter vehicle (OV), represented a compromise system that was controversial from its beginnings. Not a true space airplane, the shuttle would be lifted into space on expendable Saturn rockets. It would orbit for one or two weeks to give crewmembers time to conduct experiments. They could also place, repair, launch, or retrieve satellites. The shuttle would then return to Earth, not as a powered aircraft, but as a glider. The shuttle would simply aim down through the atmosphere with minor corrections to its angle of descent, then land on large runways. On land, when the shuttles had to be moved from one place to another, it would be placed piggyback on a Boeing 747 jet aircraft and carried as cargo to facilities for repair. Each shuttle weighed more than 170,000 pounds (77,110 kg) and was designed to accommodate a seven-member crew.

There were six shuttles built in the twentieth century. The first was named *Enterprise* after the science fiction spacecraft in the television show *Star Trek*. It never went into orbit. Instead, *Enterprise* was built to test the difficult glider landing, habitability, instrumentation, and the unique system of heat-resistant ceramic tiles that coated the craft.

The other five craft were named after great ships that had once been engaged in exploration by sea: the *Columbia*, built in 1981; the *Challenger*, built in 1982; the *Discovery*, built in 1983; the *Atlantis*, built in 1984; and

The *Discovery* was named after Captain James Cook's ship that accompanied him on his third and final voyage. It also shares the name with the spaceship from the films *2001: A Space Odyssey* and *2010*. It is now the oldest orbiter in service.

the *Endeavour,* built in 1991 to replace the *Challenger.* Both *Columbia* and *Challenger* were lost in tragic accidents. Those losses raised serious questions about the future of the shuttle program and of NASA itself. People wondered whether manned space travel was a wise idea.

THE MISSIONS

At first NASA planners had hoped that the shuttles could be used to provide a practical, reliable, and routine trucklike service to outer space. Customers could be charged for services such as placing a satellite in orbit or recovering one that was malfunctioning or had not reached its proper altitude. Several of the early missions by *Columbia* and *Challenger* were just such jobs. The estimated cost of one such

NAMING THE SHUTTLES

After selecting the name *Enterprise* for the experimental shuttle, NASA decided to name the rest of the fleet for famous sailing vessels. *Columbia* was named for a sailing boat from Boston, Massachusetts, that was used in 1792 by Captain Robert Gray to explore the region around what is now southern British Columbia and the states of Washington and Oregon. Later, the first U.S. Navy ship to circumnavigate Earth also had the same name.

Challenger was named for the British research ship HMS *Challenger.* This ship was used to explore both the Atlantic and Pacific oceans in the 1870s. The *Discovery* had been one of the two ships used in the 1770s by Captain James Cook in his explorations of the Pacific Ocean.

Atlantis was the name of a research ship owned by the Woods Hole Oceanographic Institute that operated out of its port in Massachusetts from 1930 to 1966. It was the first American ship to be used exclusively for oceanographic work.

Endeavour was named after another of Captain Cook's ships. Cook sailed *Endeavour* in 1768 to the Pacific to observe the transit of Venus as it passed between Earth and the Sun. His measurements helped calculate the true distance of Earth to the Sun (93 million miles/ 149.6 million km).

mission ran about $140 million. In order to attract business, NASA charged less—about $42 million. NASA hoped to undercut operations by the French commercial rocket service and to make its services attractive to the U.S. military and others; however, NASA was soon banned from using the shuttles to carry commercial cargo. The Defense Department announced that it would launch its expensive surveillance satellites by disposable rockets (with proven records of reliability) rather than on the shuttle. The shuttles were clearly not a moneymaking business.

Other problems with the original plan to convert the shuttles into a regular "truckline to space" soon developed. The first concepts called for as many as 50 visits to outer space every year. By the mid-1980s, planners had settled on a less ambitious but still heavy schedule of some 24 visits per year. NASA had hoped that between each flight, a shuttle would need about 10 days for maintenance and minor repairs. However, the average time for maintenance between flights was more than two months.

Critics charged that the shuttle was based on a faulty idea. It combined an aircraft/glider with vertical liftoff rockets. The rockets fell away as the shuttles lifted out of the atmosphere. The design meant that astronauts were strapped to highly explosive fuel for liftoff. They also faced a risky descent without power. Unlike an airliner, if the shuttle missed its landing field, it could not turn around to try again.

CHALLENGER

Challenger launched on its tenth mission on January 28, 1986. The crew included a public school teacher, Christa McAuliffe, who had been chosen from among 11,400 applicants. The launch was controversial. Even though Florida is generally warm in the winter, during the three days before the liftoff, the local weather had dropped severely. At launch time, it was 36° Fahrenheit (2° Celsius), some 15 degrees colder than the coldest prior launch. On previous flights in cold weather, the O-rings that joined the fuel tanks aboard the liftoff rockets had suffered serious erosion. These rubber rings sealed a flexible joint around the edges of the two fuel tanks. When the O-rings hardened in the cold and lost their flexibility, they developed tiny cracks. The cracks allowed fuel to leak out.

Engineers warned that the cold temperature could create a problem with the launch, but managers overruled their objections. They claimed that there was no proof that the temperature created increased risk. Furthermore, they argued that the schedule was important and they could not delay the launch because of supposed problems. Finally, they explained that the shuttles had operated in cold weather before and had experienced "normal" cracking of the O-rings.

Despite warnings about the cold weather by engineers, the *Challenger* launched as scheduled on January 28, 1986. Just 59 seconds into the launch, the space shuttle exploded over the Atlantic Ocean. The explosion was caught on video and immediately broadcast on television.

Challenger lifted off. Just 59 seconds into its flight over the Atlantic, the rocket assembly exploded. Debris and the crippled shuttle fell to the ocean. It took 22 seconds for *Challenger* to hit the ocean. The crew was killed instantly. The nation and the world were stunned as the explosion replayed over and over on television.

As a result, all shuttle flights were grounded for 32 months, and an investigation into the accident began. Experts testified, as did the engineers who had protested against the flight. It was agreed that the O-rings and their exposure to cold had been the immediate cause of the disaster. Deeper causes were found, however, tied to the management style at NASA itself.

Investigators pointed out that NASA had treated the shuttle as an "operational" spacecraft, rather than an experimental craft. This meant that NASA had come to rely on the shuttle to perform regularly scheduled duties. It had stopped testing and modifying it. Furthermore, when small problems developed, instead of regarding them as signs of increased risk and a need for adjustment, management often chose to regard a successful flight with one of these identified problems as proof that the problem was an acceptable risk. As commission member Richard Feynman, who had won the Nobel Prize in physics in 1965, pointed out, "NASA exaggerates the reliability of its product, to the point of fantasy." Feynman compared NASA's expectation of acceptable performance of the shuttles with the damaged O-rings to a bridge designer expecting his bridge to carry heavy loads despite a large crack in the bridge after regular usage. If the bridge designer argued that the traffic proved that the bridge was able to carry the routine load with the crack, he would be acting irresponsibly. Instead, of course, the builder would note that the bridge had failed to meet its design specifications and would recommend barring traffic until full repairs with new materials could be achieved. NASA knew its shuttles had problems. Yet, it kept launching them. Managers took the continued performance of the shuttles as evidence that the flaws did not matter.

The commission pointed out that NASA managers had become so used to thinking of the shuttles as routine and operational that it had decided that it was even safe to send aloft politicians and others to gain public support. Senator Jake Garn of Utah, a supporter of NASA, flew aboard *Discovery* in April 1985. In January 1986, NASA sent up

Congressman Bill Nelson of Florida on a *Columbia* mission. The crew on the last flight of *Challenger* had included Christa McAuliffe.

Managers at NASA demanded that engineers prove the shuttle unsafe to fly before canceling a flight. Instead, they should have proven the shuttle as safe to fly. Inside NASA, engineers had become used to deferring to management on policy and schedule decisions. All of these criticisms of the way that NASA managed the shuttle program were noted. NASA was told to fix its corporate culture.

COLUMBIA

On January 16, 2003, almost exactly 17 years to the day after the *Challenger* disaster, *Columbia* was launched on its twenty-eighth mission. Some observers noted that when the rockets lifted off their stand, large pieces of the foam covering the fuel tanks broke loose. One of them appeared to strike the left wing of *Columbia.* In an intense round of correspondence and conversations, engineers and managers discussed how important the foam breakage was. Managers pointed out that pieces of foam had broken loose many times before. The impacts had not harmed the tiles on the wing. Often the shuttles had returned with pockmarks or damaged tiles that would later be replaced during routine maintenance. Some engineers, however, wanted to test whether the foam had caused severe damage by setting up a test station while *Columbia* was in orbit. Management had the last say: There was no proof that the foam could cause a problem. No test would be funded.

On February 1, as the *Columbia* reentered the atmosphere after its two-week mission, observers on the ground watched as the shuttle broke apart. Pieces were spread in a strip across Texas and into Louisiana, covering several hundred miles. There was no hope that any of the crew survived the impact. After the *Challenger* disaster, the shuttles had been equipped with parachutes that could be used, but only if the flight compartment stayed intact until a low enough altitude to deploy them. In this incident, the cabin could not withstand the force of the breakup.

The Columbia Accident Investigation Board (CAIB) studied the wreckage and investigated the disaster. It found that the foam striking the left wing had indeed damaged the wing. A test was set up. A piece of foam the size of the piece that broke from the fuel tanks was shot against a mock-up of the wing. From the test, it was clear that foam, even though light, when traveling at several hundred miles an hour could damage the tiles severely.

The CAIB once again criticized NASA's corporate culture. The 2003 report was eerily similar to the report 17 years earlier. It pointed out the same bad decision-making processes and management style.

A FLAWED CORPORATE CULTURE

The 2003 report concluded that both shuttle accidents were caused by a failure of NASA's organizational system. Flying with known flaws had become routine and acceptable. The report noted that, "If not corrected, the scene is set for another accident."

Other aspects of poor managerial style surfaced. In the interest of saving money, NASA had contracted out much of the work on parts. It accepted contractors' own estimates of the quality of their work and did not check the quality itself. Downsizing and personnel cutbacks cut into staff, who were sent the message that efficiency and keeping to schedule were of higher priority than safety was. Before *Challenger,* NASA had 17 years and 87 missions without a serious accident. This led to a false sense of confidence. Furthermore, NASA's claim of having a "safety culture" was simply a myth that resulted in tragic consequences for the crew members and their families.

At the beginning of the twenty-first century, it was clear that NASA would need to change its management style. Space travel and exploration by manned crews, if they were to go forward in the next decades, would have to be structured in a different fashion.

7

Unmanned Space Exploration

IT IS NATURAL TO THINK OF SPACE EXPLORERS AS THE ASTRONAUTS and cosmonauts who travel into space; however, some of the most important space exploration was done by unmanned spacecraft. Space exploration puts lives at risk. For this and many other reasons, exploration by unmanned spacecraft is preferred, rather than transporting astronauts into space.

Unlike humans, the scientific equipment used in space does not require food, water, or air. Scientific sensors and cameras can be packed into much smaller spaces than life support systems needed by astronauts. Thus, a spacecraft complete with radiation-detecting equipment, cameras, computers, and radios can weigh just a few hundred pounds rather than the tons required to sustain human life in outer space. Less weight requires less expensive rockets and less fuel. So unmanned craft not only are less risky, they can be smaller and cheaper. Many of them can be sent for the same cost of sending one manned craft.

UNMANNED TO THE MOON

While Project Apollo was under way in the mid-1960s, NASA attempted several unmanned flights to the Moon. There were numerous disappointing failures and some eventual successes. In a series named Ranger, from 1961 through 1965, the first five rockets failed for many reasons. Even after a personnel shakeup at the Jet Propulsion Lab (JPL) that had designed the on-board equipment, *Ranger 6,* launched in January 1964, still had defects, crashing on the Moon without sending pictures.

Finally, in July 1964, *Ranger 7* was a success. It sent pictures as it sailed down to the Moon. *Ranger 8* and *9* in 1965 were also successes. *Ranger 9*'s pictures of the Moon's surface went directly to broadcast television, watched by millions of viewers.

In January 1966, the Soviet Union achieved an automated soft-landing on the Moon with *Luna 9*. It, too, sent back televised pictures from the surface. The American *Surveyor 1* through *Surveyor 7* made successful Moon soft-landings, sending pictures between June 1966 and the end of 1967. NASA got detailed previews that would be useful to the astronauts.

THE PLANET MISSIONS

Americans also launched numerous unmanned spacecraft to other planets. Eight Mariner flights launched between 1962 and 1975. They explored Mars, Venus, and Mercury. Two Pioneer missions followed, using much the same equipment to explore the asteroid belt and Jupiter. Most of these craft flew past their target planets, taking pictures as they went and relaying information back

The Viking explorations of Mars between 1975 and 1980 were more ambitious. The Viking crafts orbited Mars and sent back information. The craft included a lander that would descend to the surface of Mars and send back photographs and other information. A goal of the Viking explorations was to determine if Mars had ever supported life. The unmanned Voyager and Galileo flights followed.

One technique that helped in several of the later interplanetary voyages was using the gravity of one planet to pull in the spacecraft and then "slingshot" it on its way to the next destination. In 1965, an analyst at the JPL, Gary Flandro, proposed the idea to speed up what would be a 30-year straight voyage out to Neptune. He pointed out that by using the planets' gravity, a craft could reach Neptune in less time. Using planets' gravity was like getting a free propulsion system.

By studying the expected alignments of the planets in 1977, and planning ahead from 1965 when Flandro suggested the idea, the scheme allowed for a tour of the planets using this added gravity thrust. Due to cost, *Voyager 1* would explore just Jupiter and Saturn. *Voyager 2* would go on to Neptune. JPL engineers first practiced the slingshot technique. They used the gravity of Venus to send *Mariner 10* toward Mercury in 1974.

That project worked fine. The added speed in orbit past Venus allowed *Mariner 10* to orbit around Mercury three times. It took the closest, most accurate pictures of that planet's surface ever seen.

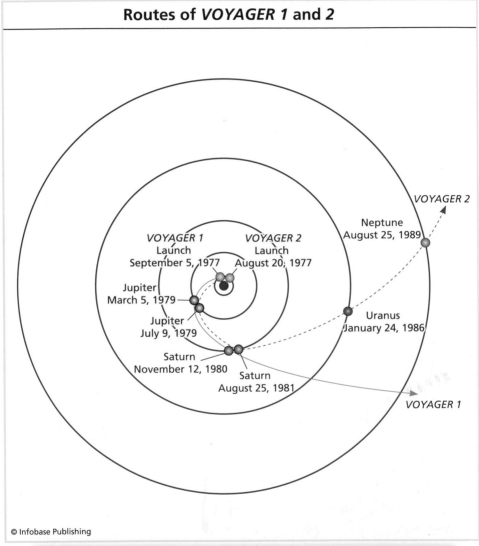

Routes of *VOYAGER 1* and *2*

VOYAGER 2

VOYAGER 1
Launch
September 5, 1977

VOYAGER 2
Launch
August 20, 1977

Neptune
August 25, 1989

Jupiter
March 5, 1979

Jupiter
July 9, 1979

Uranus
January 24, 1986

Saturn
November 12, 1980

Saturn
August 25, 1981

VOYAGER 1

© Infobase Publishing

The Voyager spacecrafts undertook the most ambitious missions up to that time: a visit to all four of the solar system's gas giant planets—Jupiter, Saturn, Uranus, and Neptune. Because of planetary alignment, the spacecrafts can visit each of these planets in just 12 years instead of the 30 years that would usually be required. Currently, *Voyager 1* is the farthest manmade object from Earth.

Astronomers and the public were surprised to learn that Mercury was pockmarked with thousands of craters more clustered than those on the Moon. One crater named Caloris was nearly one-third the diameter of the whole planet. Before 1974, the craters were simply too far away to be seen with the most powerful telescopes on Earth. Similarly, before *Voyager 1* was slingshot to Jupiter, astronomers had counted 13 moons of Jupiter. *Voyager 1* found another. After other probes by later craft, more than 60 moons of the planet have been found.

MARINER AND PIONEER

Designers of the Mariner spacecraft faced many challenges. The craft needed electrical energy to run small motors to change camera angles and other sensors. Motors also directed the angle of thruster propellants and turned the thrusters on and off. Onboard computers had to be warmed up to operate but could not get too hot. Radio signals had to be received, despite any distortion and interference from magnetic fields in outer space, and they had to be properly interpreted. Data, including visual images, had to be sent back reliably to Earth.

Each of these issues required solutions. All equipment had to weigh very little so that fuel would not be wasted. Some ingenious designs solved the problems; however, the earliest computers did not perform as expected and missions were bothered by many mechanical problems. Still, the gain in knowledge was great.

The *Mariner 3* and *4* spacecraft were 9.5 feet (2.8 m) high by 22.5 feet (6.8 m) across. Each craft carried a single camera that could take 21 pictures during a planetary flyby. It also held a system that would take more than eight hours to send to Earth a single picture. The craft carried equipment to measure Martian atmospheric pressure, a solar plasma probe, and Geiger counters for radiation measurements. They also carried cosmic-ray telescopes and cosmic-dust detectors. The position of the craft was determined by a sensor that would lock on the Sun and another that would detect the star Canopus. A small engine that could make two mid-course corrections was included. A computer and "mission sequencer" ensured each step occurred in proper order. Power was provided by more than 28,000 solar cells and by batteries.

The *Mariner 6* and *7* crafts each weighed 910 pounds (412 kg). They were built on magnesium frames, and each was 11 feet (3 m) tall. Each carried four solar panels with a total of more than 83 square feet (25 square m) of exposed panels to pick up sunlight and convert it to electrical power. The missions for both craft were to fly past Mars and to take pictures. Each Mariner carried two cameras that were mounted on platforms that could be controlled from Earth. Both crafts sent back lots of data and hundreds of pictures that gave clear close-up images of the surface of Mars.

Although *Mariner 8* failed shortly after launch on May 8, 1971, *Mariner 9* combined all the mission objectives of the failed mission with its own. *Mariner 9* faced the worst dust storm ever seen on Mars, but with control from Earth, the craft stayed in orbit. It then began its mapping and its scientific measurements in late 1971 and early 1972.

Pioneer 10 and *11* were very different from the Mariners. They were built around a 9-foot (2-m) diameter antenna that unfolded like an umbrella. At the center of the antenna was a compact set of boxes that contained experiments and equipment. Power came from two radioisotope thermoelectric generators (RTGs) mounted on booms that extended out from the equipment boxes. A third boom carried a magnetometer to measure magnetic fields. Many experiments and sensors were packed inside. These included a meteorite detector, a plasma analyzer, a charged particle detector, a cosmic-ray telescope, and a Geiger tube telescope. They also included photometers to measure infrared and ultraviolet light. The total weight of each Pioneer craft was 570 pounds (258 kg). This included 66 pounds (29.9 kg) of scientific instruments.

The missions of the *Pioneer 10* and *11* were to explore Jupiter and its nearby space. They were also to investigate the asteroid belt and test conditions out as far as the orbit of Saturn. Saturn was about one billion miles (1.6 billion km) from the Sun. By sending back the details on radiation, asteroid and meteorite particles, and magnetic fields, these Pioneer crafts transmitted data that would be useful for later flights. *Pioneer 10* came within 81,000 miles (130,356 km) of Jupiter in 1973. In 1987, it became the first human-made object to leave the solar system. *Pioneer 11* came within 27,000 miles (43,452 km) of Jupiter. It approached within 21,000 miles (33,796 km) of Saturn's rings in 1979.

VIKING AND VOYAGER

The *Viking 1* and *2* spacecrafts included two sections. One section would orbit Mars. The other would make a soft-landing on the planet to gather information from the surface. The orbiter's communication system would send the signals from the lander back to Earth. For this reason, the orbiter systems included powerful and delicate antennas designed both to pick up the signals from the surface and from Earth and to send messages back to Earth. When the *Viking 1* lander touched down on Mars on July 20, 1976, it was the first spacecraft built by the United States to do so. The Soviet Union had already landed a craft on Mars. *Viking 2*'s lander touched down on September 2, 1976. It sent data and photographs until April 1980.

Images gathered from *Viking 2* on Mars continued to reach Earth for five years. After gathering information for 1,281 Mars days, it was turned off on April 11, 1980, when its batteries failed.

The Voyagers undertook the most ambitious missions up to that time. These were the planet tours. Each Voyager spacecraft had a large, 12-foot (3.6-m) diameter antenna, always aimed back at Earth. Like the Vikings, the Voyagers were powered by RTGs. Both Voyagers sent amazing pictures of Jupiter and its moons back to Earth. *Voyager 1* took pictures of Saturn's moon Titan, then headed out of the solar system. *Voyager 2* sent pictures of the outer planets Uranus and Neptune before heading for deep space. Both Voyagers had a gold plaque mounted with a diagram showing where Earth is located in space, in case one of the craft was discovered by intelligent beings far off in the universe.

THE GALILEO CRAFT AND MISSION

Galileo worked from tried-and-true basic designs. It was built around an umbrella-shaped antenna and had RTG power sources extended out on booms. Like the Viking craft, *Galileo* combined an orbiter and a probe. The probe would drop through Jupiter's clouds.

The original plan was to launch the craft from aboard a shuttle. A rocket would then boost *Galileo* toward Jupiter. This plan had to be scrapped after the shuttle *Challenger* exploded in January 1986. The new plan called for using several different gravity "slingshots."

Galileo's new path would take it past Venus, then it would loop twice past Earth. Changing the plan to send *Galileo* past Venus required better heat protection, as the original design had never been intended for the close approach to the Sun required with a Venus flyby. This spiral path would send the craft through the asteroid belt. Scientists hoped for a close-up view of a couple of asteroids never seen clearly before. It was discovered that the comet Shoemaker-Levy 9 (SL9) would crash into Jupiter while *Galileo* was nearing the planet. *Galileo* would get good images of the comet crash.

Among the amazing pictures sent back by *Galileo* were close-up images of Gaspra-951. This was the first space encounter with an asteroid. Pictures showed a strange, irregular rock pocked with craters about 12 miles by 8 miles (19 km by 12 km). *Galileo* also passed by Ida. Ida was a potato-shaped object about 35 miles (56 km) long. Surprisingly, images showed that Ida had its own little moon, about a mile (1.6 km) in diameter. This was the first time an asteroid was found with its own moon. Astronomers named the little moon Dactyl.

THE SHOEMAKER-LEVY 9 CRASH

The comet Shoemaker-Levy 9 was discovered on March 25, 1993, by a team of astronomers. Eugene Shoemaker was an astrogeologist. His wife, Carolyn Shoemaker was a planetary astronomer. David Levy was a writer, editor, and lifelong comet chaser. Soon astronomers realized that the comet would hit the planet Jupiter. This was a once-in-a-thousand-years event. It demanded a coordinated observation program around the world. As calculations came in, excitement rose. The collision would occur July 16, 1994. Observatories lined up funding and personnel to be sure to catch the event on film.

By January 1994, the comet had broken up, appearing like a string of pearls stretched out on course to Jupiter. It was no longer a comet, but the plural *comae,* with each piece assuming a tadpolelike shape of a condensed stable core with a long glowing tail stretched behind. As the date neared, astronomers predicted that fragment A would hit the atmosphere of Jupiter at 8 P.M., Greenwich mean time (GMT).

Tom Herbst headed a team at the Calar Alto Observatory in southern Spain. On the day of impact, their computer went down a few minutes after the predicted time of the crash. This caused them four minutes of nerve-shattering anxiety. They soon had their telescope and computer back in business. They noticed nothing unusual for 17 minutes. Suddenly, they saw it. The impact happened just at the predicted spot, on the outer edge of Jupiter. Shoemaker-Levy plunged into the storms over Jupiter. It was the greatest collision in space ever filmed.

The comet SL9 crashed into Jupiter in July 1994, just as *Galileo* was approaching the planet. As the 23 pieces of the broken-up comet smashed into the planet, *Galileo* was about 150 million miles (241 million km) away from Jupiter, but it retrieved some great photos, which it relayed back to Earth.

The list of discoveries and new facts uncovered by *Galileo* is long. *Galileo*'s long list of discoveries included confirmation of lightning on Venus and sending back unique images of the polar regions of the Moon. Other discoveries included the collection of detailed chemical and atmosphere information about Jupiter and its moons. *Galileo* even discovered three previously unknown moons of Jupiter.

The unmanned explorations by the *Viking*, *Voyager*, and *Galileo* spacecrafts showed how much could be learned without putting astronauts' lives at risk, and with far less expense. Much of space exploration in the future will be through similar, but improved, unmanned craft.

8

The *Hubble* Space Telescope

ASTRONOMERS HAVE MADE OBSERVATIONS FROM EARTH FOR centuries. For much of this time, they have known that what they can see is not complete. That is because light is distorted as it travels through Earth's atmosphere. Early space advocates such as Tsiolkovsky, Goddard, and von Braun hoped for a day when rockets would be used to lift telescopic observatories into space. There, teams of astronomers and astrophysicists would be able to make startling new discoveries through the clear reaches of space. Although astronauts carried telescopes and cameras on their missions to the Moon, unmanned orbiting telescopes have made the most important observations from outer space. The predictions of the early rocket enthusiasts turned out to be right.

From 1991 to 2003, NASA launched into space four "Great Observatories." All of them were unmanned. Unlike most observatories on the mountaintops of Earth, these orbiting observatories were created to respond to instructions sent by radio. They relayed the information and images back to Earth by radio signal.

The most famous of the four Great Observatories was the *Hubble Space Telescope (HST)*. *Hubble* was an optical telescope that used two mirrors to reflect light from distant stars and galaxies. It also used a charge-coupled device (CCD), or detector, similar to the workings of a digital camera to capture images. Although there were more than two dozen optical telescopes in orbit by 1996, *Hubble* took the best pictures. It provided some of the most exciting new scientific discoveries

Owing to a small production error in its main mirror, the *Hubble Space Telescope* produced fuzzy images at first. After a servicing mission, it takes extremely sharp images with almost no background light. Observations by the *Hubble* led to the accurate calculation of the rate of expansion of the universe.

since Galileo had first aimed his homemade telescope at the night sky over Venice.

Scientists around the world proposed research projects and signed up on a schedule to be able to use the orbiting observatories. The images and information gathered by these telescopes have vastly increased human knowledge. We know more about the age of the universe, its immense size, and the processes by which galaxies, black holes, and stars have been and are being formed.

HUBBLE: A HUMBLE START

The *Hubble Space Telescope* was launched on April 24, 1990. It traveled aboard the *Discovery* space shuttle and was set up the next day.

The telescope just fitted inside the shuttle equipment bay. It was the size of a large school bus at 45.2 feet (13.7 m) long by about 14 feet (4 m) in diameter. On launch it weighed 24,500 pounds (11,113 kg). Its large 22-foot-long (6-m-long) solar panels reached out like two rectangular wings. They provided electricity to operate the equipment that used about 3,000 watts for every 97-minute orbit around Earth. An American home illuminated by 30 100-watt bulbs might burn as much electricity in one hour. To store the power, *Hubble* carried six

EDWIN HUBBLE

Edwin Powell Hubble was born in Marshfield, Missouri, in 1889. He studied at the University of Chicago and at Oxford University in Britain. In 1914, he joined the Yerkes Observatory in Chicago. In 1919, he moved to Mount Wilson Observatory near Pasadena, California, where he conducted his most important work.

Hubble studied the changes in the spectrum of electromagnetic radiation and light emitted from stars known as the red shift. In 1929, he proposed what became known as Hubble's law. It states that the farther away galaxies recede, the faster they move. He used this principle to define the visually observable portion of the universe. The radius (the distance from the center to the edge) of this sphere of space is known as the Hubble radius. Beyond that limit, objects move at the speed of light. Light or other radiation from such sources will never reach Earth and cannot be seen.

Hubble was even better known for his classification of the types of galaxies. He divided all galaxies according to their shapes. The five main types are elliptical galaxies, spiral galaxies, barred spiral galaxies, lenticular galaxies, and irregular galaxies.

Astronomers had assumed that Hubble's classification revealed that galaxies went through an evolution from elliptical to spiral. That theory has been dropped in favor of the view that one type does not evolve to another. Earth is in the Milky Way galaxy. From human perspective on the edge of the galaxy, one cannot determine the degree to which the spiral form is tightly wound.

nickel-hydrogen batteries that had the capacity of about 20 car batteries. At a fixed orbit about 380 miles (611 km) above Earth, the telescope moved at about 17,500 miles (28,163 km) per hour, or just under 5 miles (8 km) per second. Care had to be taken not to focus on or near the Sun, as the light, just as for the human eye, was too powerful for the optics.

The optics consisted of two mirrors. The primary mirror was 94.5 inches (240 centimeters) in diameter. A secondary 12-inch (30-cm)-diameter mirror had to be precisely shaped in order to focus the light from distant objects and star clusters. The mirrors were designed to lock on a distant star, planet, or galaxy and not stray more than 7/1000 of an arc second (about the width of a human hair at a distance of one mile). Expressed another way, the lenses could lock and hold on an object equal to a dime held up 200 miles (321 km) away.

As soon as *Hubble* began to observe distant objects, astronomers on the ground were disappointed. While the telescope could fix on distant objects, the images were not clear. Instead of a star showing as a point of light, the image looked like a smudge. Clearly there was something very wrong. After months of investigation, engineers traced the problem to a mistake in the manufacturing process.

The finely ground primary mirror, which had to be precise in its shape, was too flat at the outer edge. This mistake was made at the optical grinding stage. The mirror flattened out at its edges by a width of about 1/50 of a human hair. The error caused a focusing defect, or spherical aberration. The light received was supposed to come in as a point. Instead, it came in as a fuzzy-edged circle. From the beginning, it had been assumed that a maintenance mission, taking astronauts to do repairs and replacements of parts, would be needed. The *Hubble* had special handholds so that astronauts could do the work on extravehicular activities (EVAs). However, no one had planned to replace the massive and expensive primary mirror.

Engineers decided on a plan to fix a new lens so that *Hubble* could see clearly, just as eyeglasses corrected human vision. The first repair mission to correct the vision problem and to extend the life of the telescope was scheduled in 1993. Other servicing missions were scheduled for February 1997, December 1999, and February 2002.

MISSION STS-61: FIX THE *HUBBLE*

The 1993 repair mission, known as STS-61, received great publicity. Critics of NASA focused on the point that the original telescope had been sent up with a defect. They argued that the defect should have been found earlier. Such criticisms were silenced once the telescope, with its corrected vision, started sending back spectacular images from the deepest regions of outer space.

The space shuttle *Endeavour* delivered the team and the equipment for the repair. Commander Richard O. Covey, Pilot Kenneth D. Bowersox, Payload Commander F. Story Musgrave, and Mission Specialists Kathryn Thornton, Claude Nicollier, Jeffrey Hoffman, and Thomas Akers made up the team. Their mission to install corrective optics took just four hours short of 11 days and included five EVAs.

On the third day out in orbit, Hoffman, using a pair of binoculars, spotted the telescope. The crew steered *Endeavour* gently closer. Nicollier used the shuttle arm to snatch *Hubble* and bring it into the bay where the work proceeded. The optics and new gyroscopes were successfully installed and new solar panels were attached.

The mission soon met a problem that could have meant the end of the multibillion-dollar project. The hatch door to the telescope could not be closed. Specialists on the ground believed the problem developed from the expansion of bolts and other parts due to different temperatures when the hatch was removed. Two astronauts working together braced the hatch between them. They were finally able to snap it into place. There were other hitches, too. More than once, astronauts found that their space suits failed leak checks.

After mission STS-61 returned to Earth, the telescope was put through a series of tests. Scientists around the world held their breath as they waited for the first new images to come through. What they saw astounded them.

HUBBLE AT WORK

Hubble looked into the center of one galaxy, M87, located in the Virgo cluster. There it spotted a black hole that had been suspected, but never before found. In the heart of another galaxy, NGC4261, it found a disc of dust that was 800 light years across. The disc whirled around so quickly that the only explanation was that it was held in place by a black hole.

Pictured is Nebula NGC 346 as photographed by the *Hubble Space Telescope*. Nebula NGC 346 is located in a star-forming region about 210,000 light years away. With *Hubble*, astronomers have uncovered, for the first time, a population of stars that are still forming.

The black hole was calculated to be about 1.2 billion times the size of Earth's sun.

In a different direction, *Hubble* sent back breathtaking pictures of some 50 stars being born in columns of hydrogen and dust. The stars were rising out of a cloud that was itself 6 trillion miles in size. In another shot, *Hubble* found two galaxies colliding, giving off millions of stars.

Hubble looked at one small section of the sky near the Big Dipper. This area was never before explored by telescope. *Hubble* found more than 3,000 previously unknown galaxies, each containing millions of stars. The area is now called the Hubble Deep Field.

Before *Hubble,* the age of the universe was assumed to be between 10 and 20 billion years. Data from *Hubble* allowed physicists to make a more accurate estimate of 11 billion years. *Hubble* gathered hundreds of thousands of images on each orbit. It created a vast library of information that scientists would need decades to analyze fully.

COMPTON

The *Compton Gamma Ray Observatory (CGRO)* was the second of NASA's four Great Observatories. It was named in honor of Arthur Holly Compton (1892–1962). He had shared the Nobel Prize in physics in 1927 with Charles Wilson. Compton was the first to coin the term *photon.* A photon is the quantum unit of electromagnetic radiation, including light. The photon-scattering process was the basis for the gamma-ray detection instruments that were at the core of *CGRO.* The *CGRO* weighed 17 tons and was the heaviest astrophysical instrument ever put into space when it was launched on April 5, 1991, from aboard the space shuttle *Atlantis.* It orbited Earth for more than nine years. The *CGRO* was safely "de-orbited" and fell through the atmosphere on June 4, 2000.

CHANDRA

The *Advanced X-ray Astrophysics Facility (AXAF)*, later named *Chandra Observatory,* was launched in July 1999. It contained sophisticated X-ray instrumentation. Engineers expected it to last five to ten years. The *AXAF* captured X-ray images of galaxies, planets, the Moon, and other objects in space. Mirrors shaped as long tubes were used to focus the X rays. Their shape allowed the rays to glance off the interior of the tube and be reflected to a focal point.

NASA held a contest to pick a name for the *AXAF.* The winner proposed that it be named for Subrahmanyan Chandrasekhar (1910–1995). This physicist was called Chandra by his friends and colleagues. In Sanskrit, the word *chandra* means "moon" or "luminous." Trained as a physicist in Madras, India, Chandrasekhar and his wife immigrated to the United States in 1936. He taught at the University of Chicago. In 1939, he explained the evolution of white dwarf stars in his *Introduction to the Study of Stellar Structure.* He estimated that stars smaller than about one and a half times Earth's own sun would evolve into white dwarf stars. Larger stars were likely to explode into supernovae. The remaining mass could either become a white dwarf or a neutron star. In 1983, he shared the Nobel Prize in physics with William Fowler for his studies of physical processes in connection with the structure and evolution of stars. So *AXAF* became *Chandra.*

SPITZER

The last of the Great Observatories was the *Space InfraRed Telescope Facility (SIRTF).* It was renamed the *Spitzer Space Telescope.* The *Spitzer* was launched in August 2003. It was designed to work at extremely cold temperatures—near absolute zero. It took several months to cool down after launch.

NEW TYPES OF EXPLORERS

Hubble, Compton, Chandra, and *Spitzer* allowed scientists to gather vast amounts of information about distant objects in space. Just as the unmanned spacecraft explored the outer solar system, the unmanned telescopes allowed ground-based scientists to explore the universe with tools that earlier generations had only dreamed about. Scientists around the world proposed projects and examined the data that poured in from the space-based telescopes. Their explorations began to penetrate to the edge of space and time.

9

Seeing to the Beginning of Time

IN 1931, KARL GUTHE JANSKY WAS WORKING AT BELL Laboratories in New Jersey. He built a small rotating aerial, which he called the "merry-go-round." His goal was to find the sources of the static that kept interfering with early trans-Atlantic broadcasts. The aerial picked up lots of static. Jansky at first thought it came from thunderstorms or background emissions from engines. Jansky noticed that the background hiss of static on his receiver reached an intense level every 24 hours. It moved with the Sun but gained four minutes a day.

Jansky now thought the source of the static lay outside Earth's solar system. In 1932, he concluded that it was in the direction of the constellation Sagittarius. This was toward the center of the Milky Way galaxy. Other radiation apparently came from empty space. Jansky suggested that Bell Labs build a 100-foot (30-m) aerial to further investigate these cosmic radio waves. However, in the mid-1930s, it was difficult to raise funds for such a project.

THE FIRST RADIO TELESCOPES

Scientists hoped to use radio waves to explore space. They first had to meet a couple of challenges. One was the fact that cosmic radio signals are very faint. In order to gather and magnify the signals, equipment had to be both large and sensitive. Another problem was how to aim and move an antenna of such a large size. Such a telescope had to be moved to point in a particular direction in the sky. Then it had to be precisely moved to account for the motion of Earth in order to remain fixed on the point in space.

The first radio telescopes designed to sort out and register space radio signals were built in 1948. Soon scientists realized that they could gather a lot of information from radio telescopes. They could learn the strength of the signal, the wavelength and frequency, and the direction of the source.

Over the next four decades, several thousand radio sources were discovered. The Andromeda nebula, the nearest galaxy to the Milky Way, contains many stars but these stars produce no visible light. They emit only the 5.9 feet (1.80 m) radio wavelength. Other sources emit on different wavelengths. Some are a few centimeters; others are up to 65 feet (20 m) or more. A source in the constellation Cygnus was identified as resulting from the collision of two nebulae about 200 million light-years away, meaning that the collision took place 200 million years ago. Radiation at a constant wavelength of 68 feet (21 m) was discovered in 1951. It came from clouds of hydrogen in space. Some radio sources were mysterious. They pulsed on and off. These radio waves came from rotating, collapsing stars. As one huge star rotated around the other, it briefly hid the radio emission from the first. That is what caused the pulsing in the signal.

Bernard Lovell of Manchester University did some of the pioneering work in British radio telescopy. Lovell had worked in the 1930s on radar. Lovell's first radio telescope was built from 1947–1957. It had a 250-foot (76-m)-diameter dish. It was designed to bounce radar beams off the Sun and Venus. In 1957, it was used to track the Soviet Union's satellite *Sputnik 1.* It was also used to map radio wave–emitting stars, nebulae, and galaxies.

Another British radio telescope was built at Cambridge University. Rather than using a bowl-shaped receiver, the Mullard system consisted of two cylindrical structures. They were 2,400 feet (731 m) apart. One was fixed at one spot, and the other moved along a 1,000-foot (304 m) track.

ARECIBO

Professor William E. Gordon at Cornell University proposed building a large radar antenna. He wanted to send and receive signals to study the upper atmosphere, or ionosphere, of Earth. By bouncing radio signals off the thin layers of the ionosphere and reading their reflections, he hoped to learn more about the density and temperature of the region. He calculated that he would need a 1,000-foot (304-m)-diameter antenna. However, building a movable 1,000-foot-diameter antenna that could be aimed at different points of the sky would be extremely expensive and difficult to make.

Gordon decided to use a fixed antenna bowl. It would be anchored to the ground in one position, with a movable sending-and-receiving unit above it. The design would allow the beam to point in a 20-degree range around the point directly overhead. If such a device could be built close to the equator, it would be more useful. At the equator, the Sun, the Moon, and the planets would pass almost directly overhead. They would all be well within the 20-degree span of the beam.

Gordon and his team located a spot just south of the town of Arecibo in the hills of Puerto Rico. The area had small, deep valleys

The Arecibo radio telescope is set in a natural valley among the mountains of Puerto Rico, surrounded by lush vegetation. The Gregorian reflector hangs 450 feet (137 m) over the 1,000-foot (304-m)-diameter receiving dish.

surrounded by steep limestone hills. Work at the Arecibo Ionospheric Observatory began in 1963, three years after construction began. The telescope at Arecibo not only could use the radar beams to explore the ionosphere. By simply using the receiving system, the telescope could also pick up the natural radio signals of objects in outer space, including Jupiter, the center of the galaxy, and the interstellar masers and double-star pulsars.

The original cost of the observatory was $9.3 million. An upgrade in 1974 cost $9 million. A third upgrade in 1997 cost $25 million. Arecibo's main dish is 1,000 feet (304 m) across. It is made up of more than 38,000 aluminum panels and supported with steel cables. The aluminum panels, if laid end-to-end, would stretch 227 miles (365 km). The Gregorian reflector system (which uses second and third radio mirrors to focus the incoming energy) hangs 450 feet (137 m) above the dish. It is dome shaped and weighs about 75 tons. It hangs from a platform that weighs about 700 tons and is hung from 18 steel cables. The cables are attached to concrete towers that are themselves anchored with cables to the ground. Two of the towers are 265 feet (80 m) high. The third sits on a lower hill and is 365 feet (111 m) high. Even in a high wind, the whole huge hanging assembly moves only a small fraction of an inch. The cables automatically adjust for changes in temperature so that the angle and height of the platform is accurately maintained.

The observatory is the largest receiver on Earth. It allows for the study of very weak radio-emitting objects in space. The received wavelengths fall in a range from 19 feet to 1 inch (6 m to 3 cm). The frequencies range from 50 megahertz to 10,000 megahertz. With the upgrades in the 1990s, information is sent by cable to computers in the on-site research building where it can be processed and displayed on video terminals. Some of the data is stored and sent to Cornell University where it is analyzed on supercomputers. It receives thousands of visitors a year. It has even been used as background for an action sequence in the James Bond movie *Golden Eye.*

DISPERSED COLLECTION

Robert Hanbury Brown and several colleagues at Manchester University in Britain came up with a new way to study radio sources. They used several antennas, widely separated, to gain finer resolution of radio

GREGORIAN REFLECTOR

James Gregory was a professor of mathematics at the University of Edinburgh in 1663. He thought that two concave, or bowl-shaped, mirrors could focus light and eliminate distortion. One mirror would be parabola-shaped. It would have a hole for an eyepiece in the center. The second mirror would be elliptically shaped. It would reflect light back through the eyepiece hole. Although his idea made sense, the mirrors could not be built at the time. Glass grinders of the time could not make the precise nonspherical curves.

Telescopes with two or more concave mirrors to catch and focus light are made today. They are called Gregorian reflector telescopes. The Arecibo radio telescope was improved in 1997 by the addition of a two-reflector system that hangs above the main receiving dish. It uses the Gregorian principle.

sources. At first they used radio linkages between the receiving antennas and a central computer to record data. By the 1960s, very accurate, timed tape recorders were available. The researchers got rid of any links between the separate receivers and combined the signals from the tapes in a computer. This technique was known as very long baseline interferometry (VLBI). VLBI made it possible to conduct simultaneous observations at sites around the world. This concept was expanded with the development of the VLBI array of 10 dishes built across the United States. Other arrays were built elsewhere in the world.

Other radio telescopes have been built. These include 27 dishes on railcars that can be moved several miles, near Socorro, New Mexico. Other large single dishes include one at Kitt Peak, Arizona, that is 36 feet (10.9 m) in diameter. There is another more than 125 feet (38 m) in diameter at Nobeyama, Japan.

THE BIG BANG

As radio telescopes were being improved, astronomers were debating the age of the universe. In 1948, a paper described what became known as the big bang theory. George Gamow, working with fellow U.S.

physicists Ralph Alpher and Robert Herman, argued that a shift of lines in the spectrum of light from distant galaxies proved that the galaxies were moving away from each other. This meant that the universe was expanding. If the universe was growing larger, they argued, at some point in the past it must have been smaller. They came up with the idea that the universe started long ago with a "big bang."

One early problem with the big bang theory was that Earth itself was older than the calculated moment of the big bang. If the theory was true, this would be impossible. Earth might be in a steady state, with continual creation of matter. This problem was fixed when physicists recalculated the big bang's age. They now believe it happened 10 to 15 billion years in the past. Earth's age is thought to be about 4 billion years.

Radio telescopes added information to this debate. In 1963, quasars were discovered. These are extremely distant objects. They send out more energy than anything else in the universe. They are so far away that their energy had been sent out billions of years ago. Quasars suggest that the early universe was very different from the universe today. This view fits with the big bang theory.

In 1964–1965, American physicists Arno Penzias and Robert Wilson examined the sources of static that interfere with satellite communication. They used a radio telescope and receiver. Their work was similar to the work of Jansky in 1932, when he discovered the first radio waves from outer space while trying to track the source of radio broadcast static. Penzias and Wilson found a high level of background radiation at the 2.9 inch (7.3 cm), or "microwave," wavelength. It was 100 times more powerful than any known source of radiation.

Penzias and Wilson contacted astronomers at Princeton University. They found that their discovery confirmed the predictions of researchers. The microwave radiation was probably left over from the beginning of the universe in the big bang. The two Bell Laboratories scientists were given the 1978 Nobel Prize in physics for their work.

Radio telescope discoveries tended to confirm the big bang. The radio telescope astronomers and the scientists who used the *Hubble Space Telescope* represented a new generation of explorers. They seemed to travel through the universe to the very beginning of time.

10

What Lies Ahead

THE EXPLORATION OF SPACE HAS BEEN GOING ON SINCE ANCIENT times, as observers studied the night sky and tried to understand the movements of stars and planets. It was only in the twentieth century that space exploration left Earth's surface. In many ways, the twentieth century was the period of human experience where myth and dreams of the ages began to merge with technology. *Sputnik 1* launched in 1957. The flight of Yuri Gagarin around Earth in orbit happened in 1961. These events showed that the Soviet Union led the way in taking humans into space. The United States saw technology as a political challenge. It funded missions to explore outer space with astronauts. First they orbited Earth, then they visited the Moon. By the 1980s, astronauts traveled to outer space aboard shuttles.

Dreamers and engineers brought science fiction and science fact together. As they did so, they encountered criticism. Like earlier explorers, those who sought to travel in space had to fight against those who thought their plans too expensive or too likely to fail. The cosmonauts and astronauts became the popular heroes of their times and symbols of human pride and extravagance.

In the Soviet Union, Yuri Gagarin was immortalized in statues, posters, and postage stamps. He was quiet, modest, and serious—the perfect model of what a hero should be. On his death in 1968 in an airplane crash, he was mourned by millions of ordinary Russians. They loved him as much as members of their family. In the United States, the Apollo astronauts enjoyed similar fame.

Many of the former cosmonauts and astronauts have been honored by being featured on a postage stamp. Pictured is the Soviet crew Leonid Popov, Alexander Serebrov, and Svetlana Savitskaya.

In every country where space travel has been funded by the government, critics have wondered what good would come of the effort. It was fine that scientists learned more about the universe. It was fine that the United States and the Soviet Union could prove to the world that their technology was advanced. Could the money be spent more wisely to educate children, cure the sick, or provide for the elderly? After all, a fraction of the money spent on the space shuttle or on the Soviet *Mir* station could have funded many observatories on Earth and the work of thousands of researchers.

EXPLORATION OF SPACE FROM EARTH

The exploration of space from the surface of Earth has been a long tradition. It began with mathematicians and scientists in ancient Babylon, Mesoamerica, Egypt, Greece, and Rome. They came up with complex explanations for the nature of the heavens. Although some of their ideas were later shown to be incorrect, many of their observations were quite accurate.

When Galileo used the telescope in 1608 to study the Moon, the Sun, and the planets, a new era in astronomy began. Galileo and many of those who followed him were not experienced astronomers when they began to study the heavens. Galileo was regarded as someone with shocking and irresponsible ideas. He paid the price for his daring in his house arrest for the rest of his life.

Amateurs and professionals continued to build their own telescopes, improving the designs. By the beginning of the twentieth century, astronomers had discovered the eight planets of the solar system and had identified all of the major moons. They even started studying the galaxies beyond the Milky Way.

Even after *Sputnik*, exploration of space from the surface of Earth continued. These Earth-bound explorers used optical telescopes and radio telescopes. They sent unmanned equipment into space. Knowledge of space grew. Some of the greatest twentieth-century discoveries about space were made on Earth. The most spectacular discoveries came from the *Hubble Space Telescope.* Despite its initial defects, *Hubble* took pictures from light that was sent out at the beginning of time.

Many scientists argued that exploration of space from the surface of Earth had advantages. In an age when robotic equipment was being perfected, why risk sending humans to their possible deaths? An unmanned space probe did not need oxygen, food, water, or garbage and sewage disposal systems. Electrical equipment could work in unpressurized spaces, without air. It just needed a power supply and adequate design to prevent breakdown. All of the observations that humans can make—including the reading of instruments, taking of photographs, and detection of magnetic and radiation fields—could be gathered by robots and reliably sent back to Earth for study and analysis. On the other hand, no robot yet built can achieve on-the-spot decision making, inventiveness, ingenuity, and intuition found in human crews. Robotic devices have broken down in space, more than once. When this happens, their functions are lost forever.

THE MARS ROVERS AND FRIENDS

In 2003, NASA launched two robotic explorers to Mars. *Spirit* launched on June 10, and *Opportunity* launched on July 7. *Spirit* landed January 3, 2004 and *Opportunity* landed January 24, 2004, on different parts of the Red Planet. Part of a longer planned robotic exploration of the planet by several nations, the two rovers searched for and tested a wide range of soil and rocks. They hoped to uncover clues about the history of water on the planet.

Both the *Spirit* and *Opportunity* rovers landed on airbag-protected systems. They then settled onto the surface and began taking panoramic pictures. Over a period of three months, scientists on Earth studied the pictures to spot promising locations for further investigations. To conduct the tests, the rovers used quite a list of equipment, including the camera and three different spectrometers. The spectrometers tested the chemical composition of samples and of the atmosphere. The rovers also carried magnets to pick up magnetic dust particles and the so-called RAT. The RAT, a rock abrasion tool, was used to scrape the dust off samples. It allowed examination of the fresh material by the on-board instruments. Each rover was equipped with an "arm" to move instruments out to a sample.

The rovers drove from one location to another. They moved a total distance of about three-quarters of a mile every day. By moving from spot to spot, each rover acted like a human geologist. It stopped to examine interesting samples. It then tested rocks and soil that seemed interesting.

ICE CAPS ON MARS

Both the north and south poles of Mars are covered by white ice caps that expand and shrink with the seasons. Astronomers wondered if the ice caps were reservoirs of frozen water or were frozen carbon dioxide (dry ice).

The 1976 Viking missions gave astronomers some answers. At the Martian north pole, the temperatures are cold enough for water to freeze. Also, water vapor was spotted over the pole. At the south pole, the temperature is 45 degrees colder. This allows carbon dioxide to freeze. Scientists believe that the south pole has both dry ice and water ice. The permanent northern cap is about 621 miles (1,000 km) in diameter, but the southern polar cap is only about 217 miles (350 km) across. Both permanent caps are probably very thin, perhaps just a few meters thick.

In addition to the permanent ice caps, a seasonal frost cap grows at both poles. The frosty surface evaporates, with clouds of gas shifting to the opposite pole. When it is summer in the south, the moisture shifts to the north where it is winter. When it is summer in the north, the moisture shifts to the south.

Mars, like Earth, goes through long cycles of weather changes. Just as Earth has suffered ice ages in the ancient past, slight changes in the orbit of Mars have affected the climate there. These changes explain the disappearance of surface water and the changes in the ice caps over thousands of years.

Other robotic and unmanned spacecraft were scheduled through the first decade of the twenty-first century. In 2008, NASA's Messenger mission flew past Mercury. Its New Horizons mission will explore Pluto and beyond. Probes launched by Japan and the European Space Agency will help explore Mars.

THE DEBATES

All discovery and exploration has had a dual purpose. On the one hand, exploration adds to knowledge, and knowledge is its own goal. But the great explorers were also practical. They opened trade between Asia and Europe and opened trade with the New World. While some peoples profited, others paid a price. Some were enslaved, or forced to work for those who conquered them. Yet, the explorers who returned to their homes with gold, ivory, spices, furs, silk, and the other riches of the worlds they discovered were able to show that their trips could turn a profit. They produced practical benefits for those who funded the exploration.

With space exploration, the debate between science and profit continued. In the United States, the Soviet Union, and even in China, there were popular complaints that scientific knowledge alone was not worth the cost. Nonetheless, by the end of the twentieth century, hundreds of satellites were in orbit. Space enthusiasts could point to dozens of practical benefits. Some were already in place. Others loomed ahead as possible gains.

Satellites allowed for more accurate weather forecasting. This alone saved millions of dollars. Hurricane warnings, for example, allowed people to secure their homes. People could evacuate well in advance of a storm's arrival. The damage prevented and the lives saved in one storm more than paid for the cost of all of the weather satellites ever launched. Satellites also provided better knowledge of natural resources on Earth. They helped find untapped oil and mineral reserves.

For the consumer, benefits from space were often quite direct. Everywhere on the planet, people used phones that linked by satellite to the world telephone network. With world communication through telephones and television, information was more freely distributed. Information and entertainment flowed directly into the homes of millions. Even repressive governments could not completely prevent the flow of ideas.

Satellites provided military intelligence, allowing the arms control agreements between the United States and Russia to be verified from space. Military intelligence from satellites also allowed the United States and its allies to conduct very successful operations in Bosnia, Kosovo, Iraq, and other trouble spots. This information reduced casualty rates and gave commanders very precise knowledge of the location of enemy installations. Satellite information reduced the numbers of innocent civilians accidentally killed or injured during attacks on targets of strategic or military value.

Satellites also send data to the global positioning system (GPS). Small GPS devices could pick up a signal from a satellite and provide a precise readout of the location on Earth. GPS allowed for improved navigation. Scientists and environmentalists used GPS to track animal migrations and the melting of glaciers. Emergency crews used GPS to track down medical emergencies. Travelers, hikers, and explorers used GPS to find their way through remote terrain.

In this satellite image, the Yongbyon nuclear facility is seen on May 14, 2009, in Yongyon, North Korea. North Korea announced that it successfully conducted a second nuclear test on May 25, 2009, raising the stakes in the international effort to get the nation to give up its nuclear weapons program.

There are other ideas for future profits from space exploration. There are plans for mining on the Moon and on asteroids. Space travel itself is a unique experience. Planners look forward to arranging tourism in space. While the first flights carrying tourists could cost millions, space travel might eventually become routine. The cost could decline and the numbers could increase to make a regular business out of such trips.

THE NEW OCEAN

The expectations of space enthusiasts and dreamers remain high. Yet, the debates still remain. Is outer space a frontier for exploration? Or is travel beyond Earth too risky? Should space only be explored from Earth?

By the early twenty-first century, dreamers still argued for manned trips to Mars. Detailed plans for "terraforming" Mars were developed. Engineers and environmental scientists were researching ways to plant crops on Mars. These crops would help bind the windblown soil and increase the oxygen in the atmosphere. Eventually, the Red Planet would sustain human life. Science fiction author Ray Bradbury's pictures of colonies on Mars seemed much more possible and closer to realization. Serious planners looked at the costs involved in launching colonies for thousands of travelers to travel through space for hundreds of years. It could take these colonists generations to eventually arrive at distant solar systems.

The debates continue. On January 14, 2004, President George W. Bush made a dramatic proposal. It was much like Kennedy's 1961 challenge to land humans on the Moon. Bush called for a new manned space vehicle. He hoped it could carry humans to the Moon and beyond. His long-term goal was manned trips to Mars. In 2009, President Barack Obama faced tough decisions. The country was in an economic crisis. Could it afford to continue preparations for the costly manned missions to Mars? The lure of the high frontier, the new ocean, of space remains. Tomorrow's citizens will continue to debate how it is to be explored.

Chronology

1957　　　*October 4: Sputnik 1*, the first man-made object to orbit Earth, is launched by the Soviet Union. It remains in orbit until January 4, 1958.

1958　　　*January 31: Explorer 1*, the first U.S. satellite in orbit, lifts off at Cape Canaveral. It discovers Earth's radiation belt.

◆ *October 1:* NASA is founded, taking over existing National Advisory Committee on Aeronautics.

1959　　　*January 2: Luna 1*, first man-made satellite to orbit the Moon, is launched by the Soviet Union.

◆ *March 3: Pioneer 4*, fourth U.S.-IGY space probe achieves an Earth-Moon trajectory, passing within 37,000 miles (59,545 km) of the Moon. It then falls into a solar orbit, becoming the first U.S. sun orbiter.

◆ *September 12: Luna 2* is launched, impacting on the Moon on September 13 carrying a copy of the Soviet coat of arms. It becomes the first man-made object to hit the Moon.

1960　　　*April 1:* First successful weather satellite, *Tiros 1*, is launched by the United States.

◆ *August 18:* First U.S. camera-equipped Corona spy satellite is launched.

1961　　　*April 12:* Soviet Union cosmonaut Yuri A. Gargarin becomes the first man in space. He orbits Earth once.

May 5: Alan B. Shepard Jr. becomes the first U.S. astronaut into space.

1962　　　*February 20:* John Glenn Jr. becomes the first American in orbit. He orbits Earth three times.

1963　　　*June 16:* Soviet cosmonaut Valentina Tereshkova becomes the first woman in space. She orbits Earth 48 times.

1964	*July 31:* U.S. *Ranger 7* relays the first close-range photographs of the Moon.
1965	*March 18:* First space walk is made by Soviet cosmonaut Alexei A. Leonov. Duration is 12 minutes.
	◆ *June 3:* Edward White makes the first U.S. space walk. Duration is 22 minutes.
	◆ *July 14:* U.S. *Mariner 4* returns the first close-range images of Mars.
	◆ *December 4:* Frank Borman and James A. Lovell Jr. make 206 orbits around Earth, proving a trip to the Moon possible.
1966	*February 3:* Soviet *Luna 9* is first spacecraft to soft-land on the Moon.

Timeline

1958
Explorer 1, the first U.S. satellite in orbit, launches; NASA is founded

1961
Soviet cosmonaut Yuri A. Gargarin becomes the first man in space; Alan B. Shepard Jr. later becomes the first U.S. astronaut into space

1967
Gus Grissom, Edward White, and Roger Chaffee are killed in an Apollo capsule during a test on the ground

1957

1969

1957
Soviet space craft *Sputnik 1*, the first man-made object to orbit Earth, remains in orbit until January 4, 1958

1965
Soviet cosmonaut Alexei A. Leonov makes first space walk; later the same year, Edward White makes the first U.S. space walk

1969
Neil Armstrong and Edwin Aldrin Jr. make the first manned soft landing on the Moon and the first moonwalk

1967	*January 27:* Gus Grissom, Edward White, and Roger Chaffee are killed in a fire in an Apollo capsule during a test on the ground.
	◆ *April 24:* First fatality during a spaceflight occurs when Soviet *Soyuz 1* crashes, carrying Vladimir M. Komarov.
1969	*January:* *Soyuz 4* and *5* perform the first Soviet spaceship docking, transferring cosmonauts between vehicles.
	◆ *July 20:* Neil Armstrong and Edwin "Buzz" Aldrin Jr. become first men to walk on the Moon.
1971	*April 19:* First space station is launched by the Soviet Union. It remains in orbit until May 28, 1973.

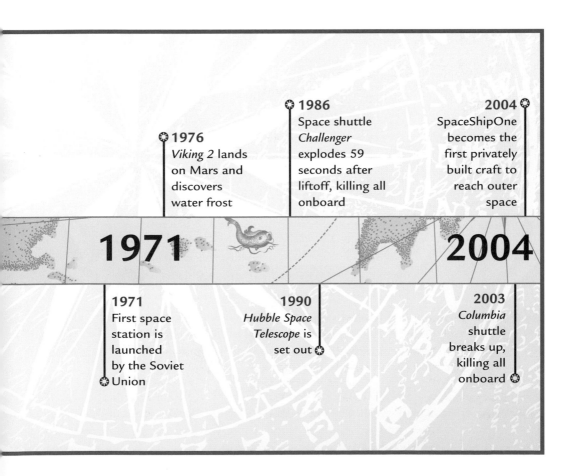

1973	*May 14:* First U.S. space station, *Skylab*, is launched.
1976	*September 3: Viking 2* lands on Mars and discovers water frost.
1983	*June 19:* Sally K. Ride becomes first U.S. woman to travel in space.
1986	*January 28:* Space shuttle *Challenger* explodes 59 seconds after liftoff, killing all onboard, including school teacher Christa McAuliffe.
	◆ *February 20:* Soviet space station *Mir* is launched.
	◆ *April:* Astronomers find that our galaxy is smaller than previously thought and the Sun is 23,000 light-years from its center.
1990	*April 24: Hubble Space Telescope* (HST) astronomical observatory is deployed.
1996	*September 26:* Space shuttle *Atlantis* returns to Earth. It brings back Shannon Lucid, the first female to crew a space station, the longest U.S. astronaut in space, and the longest time spent by a female astronaut in space.
1998	*November 20:* First piece of the International Space Station is launched.
1999	*November 19:* China launches *Shenzhou*, the first unmanned test of their manned capsule.
2001	*March 23:* Fifteen years after its first launch, and after nearly 10 years of continuous occupation by astronauts, the *Mir* space station is de-orbited, breaking up in the atmosphere and impacting in the Pacific Ocean.
2003	*February 1:* As *Columbia* reenters the atmosphere after a two-week mission, the shuttle breaks up, killing all onboard (including the first Israeli astronaut).
2004	*September 30:* SpaceShipOne becomes the first privately built craft to reach outer space.

Glossary

aberration—In optical telescopes, the distortion of an image due to built-in characteristics of the lenses and mirrors.

asteroids—Pieces of rock and ice, most of which orbit in the region between the orbits of Mars and Jupiter. Asteroids range in size from several hundred miles in diameter to the size of houses and smaller.

astrologer—A person who predicts human behavior based on the motions of the planets and other distant objects. *Astrology* is the method of making such predictions; generally regarded by modern astronomers as without foundation in fact.

astronomer—Either a professional or amateur scientist who observes objects in outer space and studies their motions, makeup, and relationships. *Astronomy* is the name of this study.

astrophysicist—A scientist who studies the physical makeup of stars, galaxies, and other distant objects. This study is known as *astrophysics.*

big bang theory—The theory that the universe began approximately 11 billion years ago with a single explosion that sent matter and energy speeding apart.

black holes—Observation from advanced telescopes that gather either visual light or other radiation have led astronomers to conclude that there are objects in the universe that are so dense that their gravity attracts all nearby objects and light to fall into them. Although not truly "holes" in the universe, but rather extremely dense objects, their effect is like that of a hole in that whole stars fall into them and disappear.

celestial—Pertaining to the heavens.

charge-coupled device—(charge-coupled detector, CCD) The key element in digital cameras that allow the registry of spots of light and the conversion of them into numerical data that can be stored or transmitted electronically. CCDs allowed the transmission by radio of clear images from satellites and space exploration vehicles.

command module—On the Apollo missions to the Moon, the command module orbited around the Moon, while the lunar module descended to the surface and then lifted off to rejoin the orbiting command module.

constellation—A grouping of stars as viewed from Earth. Since from the perspective of Earth, near and far stars may appear clustered together, a constellation may include stars that are not in a true group or cluster.

corporate culture—The habit, customs, rules, and ways of doing business that characterize an organization.

cosmic rays—Streams of atomic particles present in outer space, apparently emitted by distant stars and galaxies. When these atomic particles collide with the outer atmosphere of Earth, they generate subatomic particles that shower Earth.

cosmodromes—The launching stations for space rockets in the Soviet Union and now in present-day Kazakhstan and Russia.

cosmonaut—A space traveler, or astronaut, in the former Soviet, now Russian, space programs.

crystalline spheres—In ancient times, astronomers concluded that the planets and stars had to be held up in the night sky by some invisible substance. Claudius Ptolemy and others concluded that spheres made of a crystal substance, revolving one inside the other, could account for the fact that stars do not fall from the sky and also for their independent motions.

de-orbiting—Bringing down a satellite or spacecraft from space to Earth. When a satellite has outlived its usefulness, it is sometimes brought down from orbit to crash on Earth in a safe zone, such as an empty area of an ocean. Such a procedure is safer than allowing the orbit to gradually decay, as that could lead to a crash in a populated area.

electrical, environmental and consumables manager (EECOM)—EECOM, which formerly stood for Electrical, Environmental and Communications systems, monitors the atmospheric pressure control systems, the cooling systems (air, water, and freon), and the supply/waste water system.

electromagnetic spectrum—Oscillating electric and magnetic fields travel through space at about 186,000 miles (299,337.9 km) per second. The wavelength ranges on a spectrum, progressively

shorter from long radio waves through shortwave radio, micro-
waves, and radar to infrared light, visual light, ultraviolet light, X
rays, and gamma rays.

expendable rocket—Rockets that can be used only once to launch
satellites or other spacecraft. Expendable rockets either crash in an
ocean or desolate area, or burn up on reentry into the atmosphere.

flanges—A protruding rim, edge, or collar, as on a wheel or a pipe
shaft, used to strengthen an object, hold it in place, or attach it to
another object.

flight dynamics officer (FIDO)—The person in ground control of
space missions in charge of the craft's flight path.

flyby—Passing without stopping or orbiting. Numerous spacecraft
have conducted a flyby of a planet, asteroid, or moon in order to
gather data.

galaxy—A vast cluster of stars. Galaxies are classified by their
shape, either in the form of spirals, barred spirals, or less-
defined shapes. Millions of galaxies have been observed with
telescopes, such as the *Hubble Space Telescope,* which orbits
around Earth.

geocentric—Earth-centered. Claudius Ptolemy (ca. A.D. 100–170)
developed a model of the universe in which the Sun, Moon, and
the planets revolved around Earth. This Earth-centered solar system model is known as a geocentric model.

gravity assisted trajectory—A pathway through outer space that is
enhanced by a relatively close passage near a planet or moon to
pick up speed from the planet's gravitational field. Several manned
and unmanned space exploration missions have made use of this
"slingshot" effect to reduce the need for fuel and to extend the
reach of the spacecraft.

Gregorian reflector—A secondary, small mirror used in astronomi-
cal devices, including both optical telescopes and radio telescopes,
to bring the received waves into focus back through a hole in the
primary reflecting mirror. It is named after James Gregory, a sev-
enteenth-century Scottish professor who suggested the design.

ground control—The engineering and management staff based on
Earth that stays in communication with astronauts on manned
missions, providing analysis of information and instructions based
on that information.

guidance officer (GUIDO)—A flight controller responsible for determining the location of the spacecraft in space and monitoring the guidance systems onboard.

gyroscope—A spinning wheel or disk used for measuring or maintaining an angular position. The gyroscope works in situations when unable to use a magnetic compass (as in the *Hubble* telescope).

heat shield—A conical or dish-shaped piece of heat-resistant material, usually a ceramic, used to protect a space vehicle on its return to Earth through the atmosphere. The friction of rapid descent raises temperatures above the melting point of metals.

heliocentric—Sun-centered. Nicolaus Copernicus (1473–1543) theorized that the motions of the planets in the solar system as they appear from Earth could be better explained by a model of the solar system with the Sun at its center, rather than Earth, as presumed under a geocentric model.

instrumentation and communications officer (INCO)—The person responsible for all data, voice, and video communications systems during space missions.

intercontinental ballistic missile (ICBM)—During the late 1950s, the Soviet Union and the United States began to construct rockets capable of delivering a nuclear weapon to a target in the other nation's territory. Under arms control agreements negotiated in the 1980s and 1990s, many ICBMs have been eliminated.

interferometry—A technique used in radio astronomy in which signals from different radio telescopes are combined by computer to construct a high-resolution image of a distant object such as a star or galaxy.

ionosphere—The outer layers of Earth's atmosphere, from about 38 miles to 620 miles (61 km to 997 km) up, containing gases that are ionized, that is, whose atoms are broken down by radiation into positive and negatively charged particles.

light-year—The distance traveled by light or other electromagnetic radiation at the speed of about 186,000 miles (299,337.9 km) per second over the period of a year. Expressed another way, a light-year is equal to about 10 trillion kilometers (6.2 trillion miles).

lunar module (LM) or **lunar excursion module (LEM)**—The part of the Apollo spacecraft that descended to the surface of the Moon, then later rejoined the orbiting command module.

magnetometer—In space exploration, a device for measuring the strength or intensity of the magnetic field of a planet or a moon.

magnetosphere—The volume of space around a planet that is controlled by the planet's magnetic field, acting as a magnetic shell. The shell deflects the solar wind around the planet.

mares—The dark, relatively smooth areas of the Moon, once thought to be seas, or *mares* in Latin. Closer telescopic observation and human visits to the Moon have determined that the mares consist of dust and gravel.

module—A major section or part of a spacecraft. Space stations are often designed with numerous connected modules with different functions, such as laboratory, workshop, living quarters, and service facilities.

navigation—The science of finding one's location in reference to other known locations. Navigation is accomplished in near outer space by sightings of Earth's horizon, and in more distant space, by locating a particular known star and computing the angle between that star and the Sun.

Nobel Prize—The inventor of dynamite, Alfred Nobel, left his fortune to support the awarding of prizes in different fields of science. Beginning in 1901, annual prizes are awarded in the fields of chemistry, physiology or medicine, and physics (as well as literature and peace). Often, two or more scientists share the prize, which includes a medal and a very large cash award.

orbit—The pathway of one object around another in space. The orbit of Earth around the Sun is not precisely circular but rather a slightly elongated ellipse, with a mean distance to the Sun of about 93 million miles, or 149.6 million kilometers.

orbiter—Any spacecraft that goes into orbit around a planet. More specifically, the space shuttles are classed as orbiters. Built by NASA between 1981 and 1993, six crafts were designated as "orbiter vehicles," although only five were designed to go to orbit. Two of the fleet have been lost in accidents.

O-ring—A rubber gasket in the shape of a circle that is used to separate two parts of a machine. In the Saturn rockets used as the first stage to lift shuttles into space, the fuel tanks are separated by large O-rings that were discovered to be unsafe in extremely cold weather.

parabola—A specific type of curve, formed mathematically by cutting a cone by a plane held parallel to one side of the cone.

parsec—Measure of distance equal to about 3.2616 light-years.

payload—The net carrying capacity of an aircraft or spacecraft.

probe—In space exploration, an automated vehicle or craft that descends through the atmosphere of a planet. Probes to Jupiter are destroyed in the atmosphere of the planet, while probes to some other planets have successfully descended to the surface of the planet to conduct tests.

quasar—A contraction of *quasi-stellar,* a quasar is a starlike object found outside galaxies but that emits radiation on the scale of 100 large galaxies.

radioisotope thermoelectric generator (radio thermal generator, RTG)—A device for generating electricity from the differential heating of two adjacent metals warmed by the decay of a radioactive isotope. RTGs were used in several early unmanned spacecraft as power sources.

radio telescope—A device for receiving electromagnetic radiation from distant stars or other objects that is emitted in the radio wave part of the spectrum. Radio telescopes have been built on Earth and have been placed in orbit.

redshift—The lengthening of wavelengths from objects in space produced by the rapid movement of the objects away from Earth. The color of the object shifts down the electromagnetic scale, in the red direction, hence the name. By measuring the redshift, the speed of an object can be estimated.

retrofire officer (RETRO)—The person in ground control of space missions in charge of the timing of retrofiring rockets to slow the spacecraft.

retrograde motion—The apparent shift in the position of a planet in the night sky of Earth, from a regular forward motion to an apparent loop back in its own pathway. The apparent retrograde motion is due to the changing locations of both Earth and the observed planet.

satellite, artificial and natural—A satellite is an object revolving around a larger one. The Moon is a natural satellite of Earth. Since 1957, humans have launched by rocket hundreds of artificial satellites to revolve around Earth.

shuttle—In space exploration, any one of five spacecraft designed to be lifted into orbit by heavy rockets and to return to Earth in a controlled glide. Five operating shuttles have been constructed— *Challenger, Columbia, Discovery, Atlantis,* and *Endeavour*—in addition to the *Enterprise,* which was built to test some characteristics of the craft but not designed for orbit.

solar system—The group of planets and other objects, including Earth, that revolve around the Sun. There are nine planets as well as numerous moons, comets, and asteroids in the solar system.

solar wind—The stream of atomic particles flowing out from the Sun at speeds between 200 and 600 miles (321 km and 965 km) per second. The particles are mostly electrons and protons. Some of the solar wind comes in gusts or bursts, causing interference with cell phone and radio receivers.

space station—An orbiting facility in space, constructed by taking separate modules into space and connecting them in place, and designed to accommodate a crew aboard to conduct experiments and do other work. The Soviet, later Russian, space station *Mir* operated for about 15 years. The *International Space Station* was partially constructed by 2004.

spectrometer—A device used to analyze the radiation emitted by a distant object. The spectral information collected can be used to determine the chemical composition of the distant object and also to measure the redshift of light and so determine the speed of the object away from Earth.

stage—A step in rocket firing sequences. In space travel, rockets are often stacked so that those with the heaviest lifting capacity fire first, carrying smaller rockets aloft for separation and later ignition. The initial firing of the heavy-lifting rockets is the first stage, with later ignitions numbered thereafter.

subsystem—In engineering, a subsystem is an interrelated set of parts that perform a specific function within a larger system. Thus, for example, in a spacecraft, the atmospheric supply system for astronaut breathing will include subsystems for the removal of carbon dioxide and contaminants.

telemetry officer (TELMU)—The person in ground control of space missions in charge of monitoring information on a craft's performance and status.

trajectory—The pathway of a projectile or missile, often in the shape of a large arc that can be described as a parabolic curve.

zodiac—The ancient astronomers of Babylon identified 12 constellations across the sky through which the Sun would rise at different times of the year, and through which the planets would cross on their paths through the heavens. Each of the constellations covers about 30 degrees of the night sky, and all 12 of them lie along the horizon when viewed from parts of the Northern Hemisphere of Earth. They are Aries, Taurus, Gemini, Cancer, Leo, Virgo, Libra, Scorpio, Sagittarius, Capricorn, Aquarius, and Pisces.

Bibliography

Aldrin, Buzz, and Malcolm McConnell. *Men from Earth.* 2d ed. New York: Bantam Books, 1991.

Armstrong, Neil, Michael Collins, and Edwin E. Aldrin Jr. *First on the Moon.* Boston: Little, Brown, 1970.

Benson, Michael. *Beyond: Visions of the Interplanetary Probes.* New York: Harry N. Abrams, 2003.

———. "Celestial Sightseeing." *Smithsonian Magazine* (November 2003), pp. 64–72.

Bulkeley, Rip. *The Sputniks Crisis and Early United States Space Policy.* Bloomington: Indiana University Press, 1991.

Burke, B. F., and F. Graham-Smith. *An Introduction to Radio Astronomy.* New York: Cambridge University Press, 1997.

Chaikin, Andrew. *A Man on the Moon: The Voyages of the Apollo Astronauts.* New York: Viking, 1994.

Columbia Accident Investigation Board. *Report.* Washington, D.C.: National Aeronautics and Space Administration, 2003.

Committee on Human Exploration, Space Studies Board, National Research Council. Fogg, Martyn J. "Terraforming Mars: Conceptual Solutions to the Problems of Plant Growth in Low Concentrations of Oxygen." *Journal of the British Interplanetary Society* 48 (October 1995): 427–434.

Jenkins, Dennis. *Space Shuttle: The History of the National Space Transportation System—The First 100 Missions.* North Branch, Minn.: Specialty Press, 2001.

Lovell, Jim, and Jeffrey Kluger. *Apollo 13.* New York: Simon and Schuster, 1995.

McCurdy, Howard E. *Inside NASA.* Baltimore, Md.: Johns Hopkins University Press, 1993.

McKay, David S., et al. "Search for Past Life on Mars: Possible Relic Biogenic Activity in Martian Meteorite ALH84001." *Science* (August 16, 1996), pp. 1,639–1,643.

National Astronomy and Ionosphere Center. *Arecibo Observatory.* Ithaca, N.Y.: Cornell University, 1997.

Ordway, Frederick I., III, and Randy Liebermann, eds. *Blueprint for Space: Science Fiction to Science Fact.* Washington, D.C.: Smithsonian Institution Press, 1992.

Presidential Commission on the Space Shuttle Challenger Accident (Rogers Commission). *Report.* Washington, D.C.: Government Printing Office, 1986.

Spencer, John R., and Jacqueline Mitton, eds. *The Great Comet Crash: The Collision of Comet Shoemaker-Levy 9 and Jupiter.* New York: Cambridge University Press, 1995.

von Braun, Wernher. *The Mars Project.* Urbana: University of Illinois Press, 1991.

Weaver, H. A., et al. "Hubble Space Telescope Observations of Comet P/Shoemaker-Levy 9 (1993)." *Science* (February 11, 1994), pp. 787–791.

Wilford, John Noble. *Mars Beckons: The Mysteries, the Challenges, the Expectations of our Next Great Adventure in Space.* New York: Knopf, 1990.

Zubrin, Robert, and Richard Wagner. *The Case for Mars: The Plan to Settle the Red Planet.* New York: Free Press, 1996.

Further Resources

FICTION

Bradbury, Ray. *The Martian Chronicles.* New York: William Morrow, 1997.

Clarke, Arthur C. *2001: A Space Odyssey.* New York: Penguin, 2003.

Verne, Jules. *From the Earth to the Moon, and Round the Moon.* Rockville, Md.: Phoenix Pick, 2008.

Wells, H. G. *The First Men in the Moon.* Jefferson, N.C.: McFarland, 1998.

———. *War of the Worlds.* Jefferson, N.C.: McFarland, 2001.

VHS AND DVD

Apollo 13. Dir. by Ron Howard. MCA Universal, 1995. VHS and DVD.

Mars—The Red Planet Collection: Life on Mars; Destination Mars. Discovery Channel, Brentwood Home Video, 1996. VHS and DVD.

NASA—25 Years: The Greatest Show in Space; The Eagle Has Landed; Houston, We've Got a Problem—Apollo 13 the Real Story; Apollo 15 in the Mountains of the Moon; Apollo 16 Nothing So Hidden. Madacy Entertainment Group, 1995. VHS box set.

NASA—25 Years: Opening New Frontiers; We Deliver; Launch and Retrieval of Satellites; Satellite Repairs. Madacy Entertainment Group, 1997. VHS box set.

NASA—50 Years of Space Exploration: The Story of America's Courageous Space Explorers. Madacy Entertainment Group, 1999. DVD collection.

2001: A Space Odyssey. Dir. by Stanley Kubrick. MGM, 1968. VHS and DVD.

Star Wars Trilogy: Star Wars; The Empire Strikes Back; Return of the Jedi. Prod. by George Lucas. Twentieth Century Fox Home Video, 2000. VHS and DVD.

WEB SITES

International Space Station
http://www.shuttlepresskit.com/ISS_OVR/index.htm
Detailed site about the largest and most complex international science project in history, the International Space Station.

NASA Kennedy Space Center
http://www.nasa.gov/centers/kennedy/home/index.html
Located in Cape Canaveral, Florida, the Kennedy Space Center is the launching site for most of NASA's shuttles, satellites, and robotic missions. The site is full of information about the astronauts and those on the ground that are needed to have successful missions in space. Includes photographs, charts, multimedia, and educational tools for students and future space observers.

NASA Mars Exploration Rover Mission
http://marsrovers.jpl.nasa.gov
The Mars Exploration Rover mission is part of NASA's Mars Exploration Program, a long-term effort of robotic exploration of the red planet. The site has photographs, multimedia, event information, and links specifically for young kids, students, and teachers.

NASA Planetary Photojournal
http://photojournal.jpl.nasa.gov
Maintained by the California Institute of Technology's Jet Propulsion Laboratory, this site is an image gallery of the universe.

NASA Office of Space Operations
http://spaceoperations.nasa.gov/
This organization provides NASA with leadership and management of the Space Shuttle and International Space Station programs. They also are responsible for the management of operations related to services involving the human and robotic exploration programs.

Solarviews: Views of the Solar System
http://www.solarviews.com
A vivid multimedia site with the latest scientific information on the solar system. Includes biographies, photographs, a glossary, and links to other useful resources.

Space Telescope Science Institute: HubbleSite Reference Desk
http://hubblesite.org/reference_desk
Provides data archive and distribution for all of NASA's optical/UV missions, including the Hubble Space Telescope. *The site is home of science program selection, grant administration, planning, scheduling, and public outreach activities for the* Hubble Space Telescope.

Picture Credits

Index

About the Contributors

Author **RODNEY P. CARLISLE** holds a B.A. in history from Harvard University and an M.A. and Ph.D. in history from the University of California, Berkeley. He is a former chair and professor emeritus of the history department at Rutgers University, where he taught for more than 30 years, specializing in twentieth-century history. He is also a founding member and senior associate of History Associates Incorporated of Rockville, Maryland, a historical services firm. Carlisle has written many articles and more than 20 books on history.

General editor **JOHN S. BOWMAN** received a B.A. in English literature from Harvard University and matriculated at Trinity College, Cambridge University, as Harvard's Fiske Scholar and at the University of Munich. Bowman has worked as an editor and as a freelance writer for more than 40 years. He has edited numerous works of history, as well as served as general editor of Chelsea House's AMERICA AT WAR set. Bowman is the author of more than 10 books, including a volume in this series, *Exploration in the World of the Ancients, Revised Edition*.

General editor **MAURICE ISSERMAN** holds a B.A. in history from Reed College and an M.A. and Ph.D. in history from the University of Rochester. He is a professor of history at Hamilton College, specializing in twentieth-century U.S. history and the history of exploration. Isserman was a Fulbright distinguished lecturer at Moscow State University. He is the author of 12 books.